THE NEW GARDEN
PARADISE

DOMINIQUE BROWNING

AND THE EDITORS OF

HOUSE & GARDEN

THE NEW GARDEN
PARADISE
GREAT PRIVATE GARDENS OF THE WORLD

W. W. NORTON & COMPANY

NEW YORK   LONDON

Also by Dominique Browning:

Around the House and in the Garden: A Memoir of Heartbreak, Healing, and Home Improvement. Scribner 2002

Paths of Desire: The Passions of a Suburban Gardener. Scribner 2004

Copyright © 2005 by
The Condé Nast Publications Inc.

Condé Nast/House & Garden is represented on this book by The John Campbell Agency, Inc.

First Edition

For information about permission to reproduce selections from this book, write to
Permissions, W. W. Norton & Company, Inc.,
500 Fifth Avenue, New York, NY 10110

The text of this book is composed in Bauer Bodoni.
Manufacturing by South China Printing
Cover photograph by Aernout Overbeeke

Library of Congress Cataloging-in-Publication Data

Browning, Dominique.
  The new garden paradise : great private gardens of the world / Dominique Browning and the editors of House & Garden.—1st ed.
   p. cm.
  ISBN 0-393-05939-1 (hardcover)
  1. Gardens. I. House & garden. II. Title.
 SB465.B89 2005
 712'.6—dc22

                              2005006663

W. W. Norton & Company, Inc.
500 Fifth Avenue, New York, NY 10110
www.wwnorton.com

W. W. Norton & Company Ltd.
Castle House, 75/76 Wells Street, London W1T 3QT

1 2 3 4 5 6 7 8 9 0

Captions (pages 1–17): *Page 1:* Masses of peonies in a Midwestern garden designed by Deborah Nevins. *Page 2:* A stone amphitheater designed by English designer Dan Pearson is surrounded by a meadow of wildflowers. *Page 5:* Sarah Raven's English cutting garden reflects her love of strong color. *Page 6:* In his garden of follies in upstate New York, Paul Mayén created this stone grotto. *Page 8:* Clipped hedges of beech, yew, and pear form an abstract geometry in a Dutch garden designed by Piet Oudolf. *Page 12:* Water is a vital feature in this Provençal landscape designed by Alain Idoux. *Page 17:* This walled kitchen garden designed by Penelope Hobhouse for a client in Connecticut is beautifully functional.

Garden Book Photographer Credits
Nina Bramhall: *1, 94-95, 144-157;* Alexandre Bailhache: *2, 5, 8, 12, 184, 190-201, 234-247, 286-309, 362-363, 371-381;* Richard Felber: *6, 96, 116-127, 182-183, 187, 202-211, 310-311, 320-327;* Langdon Clay: *17, 99-100, 104-115, 128-143, 158-169, 252-265, 464;* Dana Gallagher: *18-19, 25, 64-77;* Giacomo Bretzel: *20, 78-93;* Laurie Lambrecht: *23, 40-49;* Aernout Overbeeke: *26-39;* Macduff Everton: *50-63;* Christopher Baker: *103, 170-181, 316, 352-361;* Todd Eberle: *188, 222-233, 319, 336-343, 413, 434-441;* Kenro Izu: *212, 217-218;* Chris Sanders: *214-215, 220-221, 250, 276-285;* Melanie Acevedo: *248-249, 266-275, 367, 382-389;* Evan Sklar: *312, 328-335;* Stephen Jerrom: *315;* Gentl & Hyers: *344-351;* Howard Sooley: *364, 398-405;* François Halard: *368, 390-397;* Marion Brenner: *318, 406-407, 442-451;* Robert Polidori: *408, 428-433;* Matt Hranek: *410, 459;* Jerry Harpur: *415-427;* Raimond Koch: *454-458, 460-463*

To the landscape architects and garden designers
who have created, and continually reimagine, earthly paradise

CONTENTS

Foreword

Dominique Browning

Though it is a large boast, it is safe to say that there will never be another book like the one you are holding. These pages capture the masterworks of our era's most accomplished garden designers. Turn to any page, and you have an open invitation to wander through landscapes that have never before been seen by the public—and may never be seen again. Gardens at their best are an evanescent art form, vulnerable to the vagaries of weather, the moodiness of plants, and the attention spans (to say nothing of the budgets) of their owners. It is only in a photographic record that there is any permanence to what began as an act of faith, of inspiration, of education, of judgment, of whimsy—the creation of a garden.

The gardens in these pages usually lie behind high walls, or at the end of long and forbidding drives past locked gates; they are places to which only the privileged few are invited. Gardens (and gardeners) tend to thrive in worlds far removed from press agents; the patrons of the great designers are also secluded from the general public. The editors at *House and Garden* often rely on word-of-mouth recommendations from the garden tribe: "Have you heard about the new gardens going in at…" "Can you believe such a monumental project is happening in…" "Do you think so-and-so has lost her mind with that new…" The professional designer may have a portfolio of representative work with which to attract new clients. And then again, many designers do not need a portfolio of work, as all their commissions come via friends of friends.

Of the dozens of gardens that the editors of *House and Garden* scout every season, we select only a handful to photograph for the magazine. We look for design that is interesting and inventive, for evidence of a deep knowledge of plant life on the part of the gardener, and for the telltale signs of a well-loved place. We seek designers whose collaborations with the landscape are sensitive and elegant, and whose designs are sophisticated and live lightly on the land. Even when a garden is shocking (we present some of those here) and calls into question our understanding of what makes a garden, we are looking for an integrity that carries it beyond mere shock value.

When the editors at *House and Garden* fall in love with a garden, we want to share it with the world—and so, too, luckily and generously, do the owners of the gardens. A desire to cross-pollinate, to share seed, to swap stories, to inspire or take inspiration, and, yes, occasionally to brag that your garden is the best of all possible gardens—all these are as much a part of the gardener's psyche as the desire to retreat into a private sanctuary. And so we are given permission to camp out under the trees, to trespass through the shrubbery, to set up shop in the flower beds. A garden shoot of any value lasts several days and takes place over several seasons. Photographers are selected to ensure that their particular sensibilities are compatible with the ambition and feel of a garden. Some have an architectural eye and are well suited to the geometric lines of the New Modernism; others are able to romance a bed of irises into a swoon, and capture that on film. The light must be just right—the intrepid photographer cannot miss the mists of a rosy daybreak or the long, slanting rays of the sun in late afternoon. And the garden must be right: As everyone who has a garden, or visits gardens regularly, knows, gardens are never as good the day you see them as they were last week, or will be next week.

This book has grown out a decade of scouting and studying hundreds of gardens, and comparing them with the hundreds of gardens published in the previous century. We have become aware, over the years, that we are living in a time of enormous creativity in garden design. Due to the happy confluence of several years of a robust economy and a generation of patrons who were primed to invest in their estates, there has been an unprecedented amount of activity in the gardening world. Add that to a dazzling alignment of creative design stars, and we have a period of fertility the likes of which we will not enjoy again anytime soon. And it is all captured in these pages.

We are so pleased to take the reader up the lane, over the wall, and down the garden path. After all, it isn't often that we get a chance to be present at the creation of a new paradise.

The New
Garden Paradise

Penelope Hobhouse

Here is a breathtaking view of the moods and themes of the most splendid gardens of our age, paradigms of the gardening arts at the turn of the new century. These thirty-five private gardens from around the world were scouted, keenly scrutinized, and selected by the editors of *House & Garden* magazine to recognize prized landscapes and the men and women who created them. Too often, the story of great gardens is a processional of the grand icons of each age. *The New Garden Paradise* illuminates the broader context from which the creative instincts of the designers spring. In a search for the "best," the meaning of gardens is defined, and the meaning of each garden to its owner and designer is revealed. But *The New Garden Paradise* captures more than distinctive styles. Themes and motifs embraced by our greatest designers echo the styles and truths of centuries-old garden building.

Ancient oasis gardens were refuges from the worst aspects of nature—thirst, drifting sands, and marauders. The contemporary garden is another sort of oasis—a refuge from the pressures of a high-tech, high-speed culture. The private gardens gloriously pictured in these pages show how owner and designer worked together to collaborate with nature, respecting the land and setting while also giving full, expressive rein to their own enthusiasms. *The New Garden Paradise* offers a rare opportunity to enjoy and admire extraordinary gardens that would otherwise remain the anonymous, secret havens of their owners. Each garden, whether stunningly beautiful, improbably fanciful, or even shocking in its singularity, merits deep appreciation.

To some of us the best gardens may be those in which client and designer think as one entity, creating a shared vision that results in something beautiful and real, where nature is respected as a distinct style emerges. A good example of such a collaboration is that between designer Mia Lehrer and her clients, two art collectors, in Bel Air, California. For others of us the European tradition of garden making is most important. The Belgian Jacques Wirtz and Fernando Caruncho from Spain are among the most eminent landscape architects working today. They draw their inspiration from the classical legacy, yet they are by no means stuck in the past. They offer vibrant interpretations of formality, while honoring the landscape in which they find themselves, hardly a concern of André Le Nôtre when he was laying out the grounds at Versailles. A few of the gardens included here were designed by their owners rather than by professionals. Sarah Raven in southeast England has shaped her intimate cottage-style garden as a successful combination of the beautiful and the functional.

The New Garden Paradise is divided into seven parts: The New Classicism, The New Traditionalism, The New Naturalism, The Plantsmen, Personal Visions, The Cottage Garden Reinvented, and The New Modernism. The titles speak for themselves. The new traditionalists combine a love of order with a respect for nature. The new naturalists draw many of their themes from a deep knowledge of plants' needs and an inherent interest in interpreting aspects of the site. The best of today's passionate plantsmen are represented here. More than avid collectors, they are deeply committed to matching plants to their new environments, and to studying and even visiting native habitats. It is this great respect that gives their gardens an organic quality. As the book says, "Their gardens are among the most miraculous of landscapes, improbable privatized Edens where anything seems possible." Who can resist the allure of John Gywnne and Mikel Folcarelli's garden in New England, where an extraordinary collection is overlaid with Jekyllean color schemes from an entirely different Edwardian tradition? The eccentric gardens glimpsed in Personal Visions satisfy another need. One can tire easily of gardens made by rules, so it is fun to have follies. The main criterion for success should be beauty, but this lies in the eye of the owner and/or designer. English actor Tim Curry's extraordinary Arab-style garden bowl, fanning up the slope behind his home in Los Angeles, is unforgettable. Palms, dragon trees, ribbons of ice-blue Senecio mandraliscae, and red-spiked aloes are arranged as meticulously as a stage set, with a cascade lit by Moorish lanterns. Exotic and startling, it is dramatic gardening on an exalted plane.

The modernist movement of the 1930s began as a reaction to prescribed formulas and historical themes. It reflected a love of nature and emphasized a strong sense of place. Borrowing from other art forms, it also stressed functionalism. After World War Two, Thomas Church interpreted modernism in his own way, and thus became its most famous and successful practitioner. He worked on the West Coast, where he built gardens to suit ranch-style houses and created the so-called "California style." It is telling that all of the gardens chosen to represent new modernism in this book are located in California, where their designers are immersed in horticultural craftsmanship. They integrate house and garden in one flowing design, and also stress the notion that gardening is more than a recreation: Indeed, it's an enrichment of our everyday lives.

Isabelle Greene, from Santa Barbara, believes her role is to work with the existing landscape, enhancing it rather than manipulating it. She furthers her thoughtful schemes by using regional plants that are at home on the site. Ron Herman's passion for Japanese culture has led him to use minimalist planting schemes that allow him to adapt classical Japanese styles to the climate of California. Roger Warner faced a different challenge in the Napa Valley: to make an informal naturalistic garden surrounded by the geometry of the vineyard layouts. As a plantsman he learned to be selective and to use fewer varieties in creating his effects.

While *The New Garden Paradise* is not a search for novel schemes or exciting new materials, it does shed light on the innovative thoughts and styles of the participants. The designers speak for themselves as they describe creating their own brand of design and the reasons and traditions behind it.

Uplifting and enlightening, *The New Garden Paradise* illuminates a grand diversity of styles while capturing the splendid passion with which our contemporary garden builders celebrate nature.

PART ONE THE NEW CLASSICISM

PART ONE INTRODUCTION

Too often, it is just a reaction. A period of extravagance has run its course and you awaken with the horticultural equivalent of a hangover. You are overdrawn at the bank, a little ashamed, and sick at the thought that once again you have gorged on flowers of questionable hue or shrubs with variegated foliage. You resolve to purge your garden of excess and become a classicist.

The impulse doesn't last and within weeks you are back to trolling the garden centers. Why? Because classical style requires discipline, devotion, and above all restraint. Classicism is a marriage, not a fling.

Your art history teacher told you about balance, harmony, and unity. What she may have neglected to say was that the ancient Greeks also loved bright colors. They painted and polished their temples and statues like teenagers with makeup. It was nature and time that had the good taste to strip the walls to a chaste marble white, and to patine the statuary with a subtle greenish black. As custodians of the natural, as gardeners, we should take the hint.

We need to draw our classicism from the intrinsic simplicity of nature. This was the hallmark of Greek classicism that allowed it to improve with age. The columns were stone copies of the trunks of

PREVIOUS PAGES
At Mas des Voltes on the Costa Brava, Fernando Caruncho has reinterpreted the classical garden, drawing on the regional agricultural landscape to create graceful patterns of wheat, olives, cypresses, and turf.

OPPOSITE
Clipped evergreens are a standard element of the classical garden; German designer Ludwig Gerns's "cloud pruning" gives a lighthearted twist to this traditional standby.

trees, the porticoes man-made groves where people could find shade during the heat of the day or take shelter from a storm. The mathematical relationships the Greeks used to set the proportions of their buildings and their art were nothing more than the ancients' efforts to formalize what they observed in nature's beauties. More than two thousand years later, their work, with all the decorative elements worn away, feels fresh and appropriate.

The exquisite clarity of a Jacques Wirtz garden may prove to be the right antidote for the gratuitous complications of daily life. Wirtz himself, still hard at work in his eighties, finds catharsis in his garden making. He explains that, in each new landscape he and his sons undertake, "we create tension, then we release it. Like music. Like a Bach fugue."

Spanish designer Fernando Caruncho is explicit about his debt to classicists of the past. A former philosophy student, Caruncho cites the Athenian philosopher Epicurus as a major influence. Maybe it was the Epicurean belief that nothing comes of nothing and that change is the rearrangement of persisting bodies that prompted him to select indigenous agricultural crops as materials for a trio of gorgeous and sensuous landscapes on Spain's Costa Brava. As Caruncho might tell you, the pursuit of pleasure (together with the avoidance of pain) is the goal of an Epicurean life.

Classicism, however, should not—and cannot—be limited to the pursuit of an ancient ideal. It must be reinterpreted for our times. A classical design must be drawn from the surroundings and assembled from local elements like the rhythmic hedges that the Belgian Jacques Wirtz plants from the native beech, yew, and hornbeam, so that it fits nowhere else. Its fundamental focus is the land itself. Douglas Reed's primary challenge in designing a client's 11-acre estate in eastern Long Island was how to repair the century-old mistake that had perched a house thoughtlessly on the high ground. Only by demolishing the house could he and architect Salvatore LaRosa

free up "the earth and space and sky," so that a central valley emerged as the pivot. With that drastic but essential step, Reed recalls, "everything else moved around the valley."

One secret of successful classicism is to limit the landscape to a few strong elements, keeping the themes clear and bold. Often, this is accomplished through an explicit geometry, as when Caruncho carefully marshaled cypresses to recall the columns that the Greeks designed to recall trees. But the classical designer of today is also free to abandon mathematical rigor. In a Long Island garden, Reed brought an informal pasture style of planting right up to lap at the foundations of the house, deliberately playing on the contrast of free-form nature with the stark rectangularity of the home the clients had built to replace the one that had been demolished.

Classicism need not be pompous. There is a light touch to Wirtz's version, an air of innocent fun in the G-clef pattern he worked into the hedge of a client he had met at the symphony. Nor is classicism, when properly understood, static. It is easy to think of a successful piece of classical design as being timeless, but that is missing the point. Rather, like those Greek temples, the classical garden works with the fourth dimension of time, acquiring power from time's passage. As Fernando Caruncho explains, the garden,

ABOVE
By wrapping the stark geometry of the house in a luxuriant fabric of lawn and wood, Douglas Reed evoked the classical in an unconventional fashion.

changing with the seasons and the years, growing and dying, inevitably becomes "a memory of time and space." The garden is the place where past, present, and future meet.

For the late Dan Kiley the garden was a means to resolve contradictions and find unity in apparent chaos. The style of his work—linear, abstract, and minimalist—earned him a place as one of the very greatest of modernist garden designers. In its mood and aspirations, though, Kiley's design was intensely classical, which may explain its enduring popularity and accessibility. Kiley believed strongly that the garden should be a force for integration, not only uniting the different elements of the landscape with the house, but also linking the whole project to its setting through the skillful use of local materials and themes. He was a master of using trees architecturally, yet he relished the details that defined the trees as plants: the smooth gray skin of a beech's trunk, or the lacy shadow cast by a locust's foliage. By the time Dan Kiley created this garden, he had long since absorbed the classicist's devotion and restraint. He may have been very much the modern man, but it is not at all difficult to have imagined him planting porticoes on the Acropolis.

OPPOSITE

Lily ponds, meticulously lined with pale stone slabs, furnish a contemporary take on the classical parterre in the garden Fernando Caruncho created for a seaside site at S'Agaró, Spain.

JACQUES WIRTZ

Belgium

While he may begin his drawings with a pencil, Jacques Wirtz transcribes his fine line in the garden with a hedge. It is his trademark: the sweeping, interweaving files of clipped greenery that work dazzling transformations on the Belgian landscape. Wirtz is a master of this simplest of elements, using it to coax out the hidden drama from these undulating fields. He understands the excitement of the subtle.

Like a skilled draftsman, Wirtz also knows how to adapt his art to suit different circumstances. Although the two gardens featured here might seem to share much—set on similarly sized plots with comparable topography—the houses to which they are married are quite different. One is a modernist villa, the other a sixteenth-century château. The result is two gardens composed of similar devices that produce profoundly different experiences.

Wirtz's art shares much with the music he listens to as he designs. His tastes are broad, ranging from Bach to Brubeck. He has compared his work to musical composition and he feels that his gardens have the same abstract power. In a rational, ordered exercise, he builds sensation, piece by piece, to arouse a strong emotional response.

No doubt it was this method of attack that attracted the client with the modernist villa. An art collector who lives in the Flemish Ardennes, the patron first encountered Wirtz at a classical music concert. Wirtz recalled this meeting, too, in the garden he subsequently created for the collector. The beech hedges that swirl up around the house form an enormous G clef.

The site was unusually spacious for this densely populated corner of the world: 37 acres of what had once been a Renaissance hunting preserve. Although the expanse of land was a rare opportunity, it was also a challenge, for it boasted no strong natural features—no cliffs or ravines or rivers—that might help organize the property. So Wirtz introduced his own palisade at the entrance, an allée of limbed-up trees, a hedge writ large, that lines the drive and forces the visitor's eyes straight ahead as the blinders on a horse do. He then wrapped hedges around the house, which is set up on a slight rise, to control the views.

"If you have the opportunity to make a bold stroke, you have to do it," advises Wirtz. In all, he planted more than four miles of hedges in this garden, a staggering total that you might think would ensure monotony. But thanks to the designer's flair in handling this element, the visitor is struck with dramatic differences from one area of the garden to another.

Near the house, the living walls are composed of beech or boxwood. Wirtz swept the beeches around in tight parallel curves, as if he had stroked the land with a giant comb. The walls define a tight series of paths and are just the right height for the garden's owners to watch their grandchildren's heads bob along as they race around this labyrinth. As the lines of beeches spin away from the house, they spill down the slope, flowing around mature fruit trees, then fan out to meet a skein of hawthorn hedges. The hawthorn is a gesture to local agricultural tradition, which for centuries used it for living fences. Wirtz sends his beeches out to explore the swells and dips of the surrounding fields and woods and to lace his garden into its setting.

A landscape of understated power, this garden has its seasonal pleasures: the flowers of the hawthorns in late spring, followed by

ABOVE

Sweeping out from the house in parallel lines, Wirtz's walls of shrubbery explore and emphasize every dip and swell of this understated terrain. Living columns anchor the hedges' ends.

"If you have the opportunity to make a bold stroke, you have to do it."

—JACQUES WIRTZ

the ripening fruits; the coppery color of beech leaves as they cling to the gray twigs in winter. "If a garden does not have expression during the winter months," says Wirtz, "it is not a good garden."

For the château, Wirtz conceived a very different style of garden, one that played on both the period of the house and that of the existing landscape, which was in a nineteenth-century "English" style. Near the house, which is surrounded by a moat, Wirtz arranged classic garden elements such as a rose arbor and courtyards enhanced with pleached trees—trees whose branches have been interlaced to make living architecture. Outside the moat, he returned to his hedges, which in this context was historically authentic. The château's original builders had no doubt planted a symmetrical knot, or broderie, a parterre of low, clipped evergreen shrubs. In his own design, Wirtz integrated an exuberant derivative of this, an asymmetrical arabesque sculpted from yew and beech, with hints of buttresses, towers, and crenellation clipped from the foliage. Taller hedges enclose and hide the greenhouse and potager. Twin bosques (formalized, rectangular woods) were made from hornbeams planted in quincunxes, or geometric groupings of five, a pattern that brings the trees close enough that their branches run into one another. They are trimmed back around the exterior to create what look like floating blocks of greenery.

As a backdrop for these sculptural features, and to define and enclose the garden, Wirtz pushed up a long, sinuous berm of earth, which he clothed with a dense growth of beech and topped with pleached lindens. He parceled the area embraced by the berm into pastures with hawthorn hedges; he dotted the pastures with shade trees to give a sense of scale. In summertime, guests can row across the moat and then climb up to a gazebo atop the berm to enjoy a cool drink and admire the view of the old château.

Wirtz believes that a garden must have a sense of mystery, that its enjoyment must be a discovery. Perhaps this is why the best season in which to savor his compositions is the winter, when the hedges slip in and out of the mist, covering the Flanders fields like great snakes, the leaves of the beeches gleam a brassy red, and the evergreens are darkly lush. As the art collector client says, "We hired Jacques Wirtz to design our garden because we wanted a masterpiece."

OVERLEAVES

Pages 30–31: *Below a château in eastern Flanders, steps of blue limestone provide a formal invitation to a suitably elegant tapestry of yew. Squared masses of hornbeam serve as gatehouses to the pasture beyond.*

Pages 32–33: *January mist wraps the landscape of the former hunting preserve in mystery. The tower atop the house provides a vantage point from which to admire the tracery of Wirtz's planting.*

Dotting distant pastures with shade trees to provide a sense of scale, Wirtz then embellished them with hedges of hawthorn, a whimsical transformation of a planting commonly used to edge local farms.

OVERLEAVES

Pages 36–37: *Hornbeams planted in geometrical patterns, their canopy trimmed into floating blocks of greenery, become a stylized woodland or bosque.*

Pages 38–39: *A rose arbor stands guard at the entrance to an allée in Jacques Wirtz's landscape for a Belgian château; crenellated hedges of beech flank the pavilion in back.*

DOUGLAS REED
New York

Douglas Reed made the trees dance. Or perhaps it would be more accurate to say that he released them, that he set them free to do what they had wanted to do all along. What he accomplished in this Long Island, New York, garden surely disproves the popular conception that classicism must be stiff, that it is only compatible with a Versailles-style formality. There could not be a less formal—or more elegant—garden than this.

The commission began with a call from architect Salvatore LaRosa. He had been contacted about building a house by a couple who had recently bought an 11-acre property in East Hampton. LaRosa was excited by what he had seen and called Reed immediately after his first visit to the property. "Doug," LaRosa said, "we will not have another site like this in our careers." LaRosa knew that if the house were truly to be integrated into the landscape, the design of the garden should proceed in step with his design for the house.

It was, in the most literal sense, a historic opportunity. The property was a remnant from a more gracious era, one in which vacation homes in this fashionable locale were given room to breathe. It had been developed as a summer retreat in 1898, and extensively planted at that time, so that when Reed traveled out to make an assessment of the property, he found more than a hundred century-old trees.

The topography, equally remarkable, consisted of a long valley that focused on a striking knoll at its western corner. Even the soil was good. The only flaw on the site was the existing house. Much

"My main goal was to take clues from the existing structure of the grounds."

—DOUGLAS REED

altered over the decades and in poor repair, it was unattractive and, what was worse, had been poorly sited. The original owners had set the house on the crown of the knoll, where the building and a swimming pool bore down on and flattened what should have been the landscape's outstanding feature. Fortunately, the clients had already decided to replace the house, and LaRosa had identified a far better setting across from the knoll on the property's eastern corner.

The clients had a taste for modern architecture, and LaRosa gave them a graceful but austere house. Reed had the good sense to react to this structure counterintuitively. Instead of designing the landscape in an angular modernist mode, he adopted a flowing and lyrical line reminiscent of a traditional English country house garden. This style suited the curvaceous character of the site and made a complementary setting for LaRosa's architecture.

Another aspect of the country house style Reed chose to adopt was that of treating the house with respect. Instead of hiding it behind foundation plantings, he set it on a pedestal, with a grass terrace edged in stone, so that the striking structure would be the garden's central feature. It became a glass, steel, and masonry sculpture. Reed and LaRosa also collaborated on water features that enhanced the interconnection of indoor and outdoor spaces. A reflecting pool lined with black stone passes through the house at the intersection of the living and dining rooms and then emerges outside where it sits in a sculpture court. In similar fashion, a fountain passes through a wall to spill down through the stepping-stones that give access to the pool house. Finally, Reed established a further link to the house with the minimalist style of the fence that encloses the pool. It is a sinuous line of stainless-steel rods—just posts, no railing—that echoes the close-set trunks in a nearby dense grove of sassafras trees.

Reed worked with the trees to reinforce and refine their effect. He pruned limbs to sharpen their sculptural presence and to create shadows on the lawn. On a practical note, he thinned the tree canopies to increase the amount of sunlight that filters to the lawn below, thus allowing the grass to grow better. In addition, he began

a planting program and added another hundred trees to the landscape. The new plantings included specimens of species already on
the site, such as beech, maple, sassafras, and tulip trees, but also
trees of other types—river birch, katsura, and cork, for example—
that would provide year-round interest with the texture of their
bark and the colors of their fall foliage.

Visitors are prone to ask where the garden stops and the wilder
landscape begins. "That is my favorite compliment," Reed says.
"My main goal was to take clues from the existing structure of the
grounds." Reed used those clues to create something quite remarkable: following their lead, he unearthed and released a life that no
one suspected was hidden in the overgrown estate.

You cannot visit this place now, the wife says, without feeling it.
A former dancer and now a patron of that art, she speaks of the
choreographers who have come to the house as guests. All of them,
"like Twyla [Tharp] and Merce [Cunningham], are impelled to
make a dance on this place. Twyla envisioned an audience on the
knoll, with the house as backdrop; Merce, the reverse. It's safety
versus wildness," she explains, referring to the contrast of house
and garden. "Opposites make people's imaginations travel."

ABOVE
*The window frames the beech tree
and emphasizes its sculptural quality.*

LEFT AND ABOVE

*A wall-through fountain continually
replenishes the swimming pool; to
reach the pool house, the visitor must
walk on water, crossing on the file of
inset paving stones.*

DOUGLAS REED • 45

The fence of close-set stainless steel rods that encloses the pool area echoes the house's minimalist style and the trunks of the nearby grove of sassafras trees.

ABOVE
Treating the house as the garden's central feature, Reed set it on a pedestal, a grassy, stone-edged terrace uncluttered by foundation planting.

RIGHT
More than one hundred century-old trees adorn the old estate, but it was only with the redesign that their true beauty became apparent.

DAN KILEY
Connecticut

The clients were quiet, private people, so they valued Dan Kiley's exuberance all the more. Though in his late 80s when he designed this garden, Kiley was still prodigal with his talents, tossing off new concepts the way an arc welder throws off sparks. "Dan had more ideas than any young person," the client confided. "He had one every minute—if not more."

A legend of American landscape architecture, the late Dan Kiley was one of the Young Turks who brought modernist design to the United States, outraging and then captivating the public by breaking with tradition. What his early detractors usually missed, however, was that Kiley's work, though it rejected the styles of his parents' generation, did have its own historical antecedents. Kiley had no patience with the borrowings of the early 20th-century Beaux Arts designers, who might graft an Italian Renaissance palazzo onto a Hudson River Valley bluff, then wrap it round with an English country house garden. Kiley was always original, but he studied and absorbed the achievements of the past. In his elegant, stripped-down style, he was, in his own way, a true classicist, though one who might have felt more at home in Stonehenge's spare stone circle than in the complex rhythms of the Roman forum.

Kiley was a consummate artist, but also a craftsman, responsive to the needs and desires of his clients. His first reaction when shown the property of this Connecticut couple was to insist that their brand-new house be painted another color: Kiley objected to its brown cedar siding, which made it look like an oversized cabin. With a coat of white paint, it would become a proper New England

farmhouse. The clients graciously accepted his directive, then asked Kiley to pull into a rational whole all the elements of the several-hundred-acre estate—entry court, service area and tennis court, guesthouse, woods, and vegetable garden. The local landscape vernacular was one of the tools Kiley intended to use to this end.

Kiley recognized that his clients were not Yankee farmers. They wanted a more formal way of life, and he accommodated them by giving the landscape a certain rigor. Trees were clipped and pruned, their silhouettes simplified and given an artificial polish. Kiley punctuated the landscape with sheared, spindle-shaped hornbeams, ornamental bosques, and allées, and framed the terrain with canals. He focused the view from the terrace on a fountain, a symmetrical peak of water that in the evening could be lit from below, following the horizon of the Berkshire Hills. Kiley had certainly seen all of these features in the formal French design that he admired, but this was no mere borrowing. He had absorbed the way in which French landscape designers such as André Le Nôtre, and the Italians and ancient Greeks and Romans before them, had used plants in an architectural fashion. With a characteristic twist, he turned their ideas to his own ends.

In part, Kiley's technique was provocative. He found drama in the juxtaposition of man's sense of geometry with the free forms of nature. Simplification was essential to his success—the clean, uninterrupted lines he gave to a wooden jetty, posing it as an unadorned "T" of wooden planking, made it a startling challenge to the meander of the lake shore. Yet Kiley did not forget that his mission was to integrate the property, so he offered a compromise. He lined the water's edge with weeping willows, a curvaceous tree that most designers avoid because its natural form is, paradoxically, so artificial. The willows marry the artificial to the natural contours of the water's edge.

Kiley's orchestration of the plant material was not so much architectural as sculptural, which served as yet another means for

ABOVE

Simple and unadorned, the wooden jetty nonetheless plays a role in heightening the drama of the garden, posing a provocative challenge to the natural contours of the lake.

integration. With his weeping willows and topiaried hornbeams, he was setting a stage. The clients were collectors and wanted to display three sculptures—works by Barbara Hepworth, Joel Shapiro, and Bruce Nauman—in the garden. Kiley was determined not to treat these sculptures as garden ornaments, since they were far too strong. Rather, he sought to integrate them into the landscape, making natural features of them.

Kiley worked two of the sculptures into the terrace adjoining the house. He found that the Joel Shapiro piece, a joyous abstract work that seems to be kicking up its heels, needed the human scale it would get by an association with the house. It would be lost, he felt, if ostracized in the middle of a lawn. Instead, he tucked it into a corner of the terrace, where it seems poised to leap over a zigzag of a stone bench and off the edge of an ivy-clad retaining wall, turn a cartwheel maybe, and run away, leading a chase through the surrounding woods.

Kiley was challenged in a different way by the Barbara Hepworth sculpture, *Two Figures*, which he saw as an intermediary piece— too strong to include in the terrace, but effective as a point of transition from the domesticated to the more natural spaces. To accommodate this work, he built off the terrace a separate platform by which he cantilevered the sculpture into the meadow beyond. Standing there, the piece remains a part of the view from the terrace, but is also projected into the views from several other angles, so that it knits together the greater area.

The last of the three sculptures, Bruce Nauman's *Trench, Shafts, Pit, Tunnel, and Chamber*, is also visible from the house, but is set farther away so that it is not, as Kiley put it, "of the house." Instead, it serves as a focal point and a destination in the garden experience, though Kiley also used it as a mediator between lake and mountains. The piece not only recalls the hills, with its angular forms and earthy, rusted surface, but also mimics the lake in the broad, bottomless basin it holds up to catch a piece of the sky.

Kiley insisted that all three sculptures were integral to his design. Had they not been available, he said he would have had to find other structures—pergolas or fountains—to occupy their positions. The garden was a series of puzzles, he argued; it integrated the formal, abstract elements into the New England vernacular— farmhouse, orchard plantings on the grid, grassy pastures, the straight lines of crops. "Every day," he explained, "we work on these puzzles, and we work it out. It is a discovery." It was a discovery in which, for more than six decades, Kiley never lost his delight.

The serpentine retaining wall at the rear "goes out and embraces the land," Kiley said. He set the Barbara Hepworth sculpture, Two Figures, up on a platform as a counterpoint to the landscape.

OVERLEAF
Kiley's admiration for formal French design emerges in this fountain, which is lit at night to make a glowing peak of water, a luminous mimicking of the distant Berkshire Hills.

ABOVE
Bruce Nauman's Trench, Shafts, Pit, Tunnel, and Chamber *echoes both mountain and lake.*

RIGHT
Though originally planned for display at the far end of the lawn, this Joel Shapiro sculpture enjoys a human scale that persuaded Kiley to pose it nearer to the house.

OVERLEAVES
Pages 60–61: *White columns of birch trunks stand like a portico before the house, evidence of Kiley's ability to absorb and then re-express in his own way the traditions of the classical past.*

Pages 62–63: *To create a view and draw the eye, Kiley cropped a panorama, framing it with this pair of mature copper beech trees.*

FERNANDO CARUNCHO
Spain

You would know this garden with your eyes closed. There is the characteristic perfume of the place—the sweet, astringent scent of three acres of lavender that is the garden's heart—and the characteristic sound from tens of thousands of bees hard at work harvesting nectar. Intentionally, they are doing the designer's work, for this garden, like all of Fernando Caruncho's work, is about man's partnership with the land. That is what makes the gardens of this most sophisticated man so distinctive: the means by which he communicates are absolutely simple.

Today, the theme of the harvest seems an obvious one for Mas Floris, a garden on Spain's Costa Brava that was one of Caruncho's first commissions. The garden was built on the site of a former farm. But the decision to return this site to fruitfulness was not at all obvious in 1983, and was a bold leap for the 23-year-old novice. Turning his back on the flowers and shrubs of the nursery, Caruncho decided to limit his palette almost entirely to local agricultural standbys. He replanted grapes in the traditional geometrical spacing of the vineyard, dividing them into four quadrants, each of which he outlined with cypress trees, which local farmers had traditionally used as a windbreak. The cypresses stood almost shoulder to shoulder in the central avenue that divided this rustic parterre down the middle. As the allée proceeded across the adjoining lawn, the interval between the trees increased. Here, Caruncho arranged the trees like "monks marching into the woods." They establish a rhythmic cadence as they mingle with magnolia trees, the only exotic plant that Caruncho allowed himself to use.

OPPOSITE
Working in the vernacular, Fernando Caruncho used the local cypresses to create this colonnade at Mas Floris, thus pulling the gaze to a marble work by Catalan sculptor Javier Corbero.

"I think of the garden as *una caja de luz,* or box of light, turning with the elements like a kaleidoscope."

—FERNANDO CARUNCHO

As you move beyond this open area, the garden becomes even simpler and more subtle. A gravel path takes the visitor into the carefully groomed wood—throughout which Caruncho has placed the client's extraordinary collection of sculptures—then out to the bees' lavender field. The cypresses reappear here, standing witness around the field with oversized terra-cotta pots at their feet.

Caruncho remains preoccupied with an agricultural vocabulary. A former student of philosophy, he also draws inspiration from his study of the ancients. "Just as in the time of Epicurus [a fourth-century-B.C. Athenian philosopher], one way to express philosophy today is through the design of gardens that incorporate the natural elements: earth, wind, fire, and water." The emotional impact of Caruncho's gardens suggests, however, that there is also a strongly visceral component to his work. In the age of the microchip, this dapper, urbane man has reconnected us with the power and beauty of the countryside. He has found in the timeless cycles of the farm an order that, as postmodern city folk, we envy.

Undoubtedly, the cyclical nature of agriculture is a large element in what attracts Caruncho to landscape design. He insists that he does not believe in the Western concept of linear time. He calls time "a labyrinth in three dimensions." That seems to be what he was exploring in the second of his agricultural gardens, Mas des Voltes, which is also set back from the Costa Brava.

This garden centers more mysteriously on mirrors: an arrangement of four rectangular pools whose reflective surfaces watch the daily passage of the sun. Planted thirteen years after Mas Floris, Mas des Voltes shows a greater assurance and a growing formality. There are the borders of cypresses again, blocks of grapevines banked up around the edges of the pools, and platoons of gnarled olives to balance a parterre of wheat. When the concept of the parterre was invented, it was envisioned as a quiet place, a refuge from the mundane. The parterres at Mas des Voltes suggest that paradise lies in the agricultural terrain from which our ancestors fled.

Besides, the wheat is beautiful—in the spring, when the green

blades poke up from the ground; in the summer, as the wheat ripens to gold; and then, after harvesting, as huge cylindrical bales recline on the stubble. To close the cycle, Caruncho has these plowed back into the soil every winter.

The fields are not the only landscape that Caruncho celebrates. He built the water garden of S'Agaró twenty miles from Mas des Voltes, on a cliff overlooking the Mediterranean. For this he used the natural elements of the shore: an embrace of umbrella pines (*Pinus pinea*) and five massive basalt boulders set around a complex of rectilinear lily pools. Light brings this garden to life: light from above, light reflected from the water of the pool, light interrupted by the shadows of the rocks. "I think of the garden as *una caja de luz*, or box of light, turning with the elements like a kaleidoscope."

This dynamic character is common to all of Caruncho's gardens. What begins as a predictable experience—a stroll through carefully marshaled vines and trees, or around the margin of the pool—turns fluid and exciting as the visitor becomes caught up in the subtle detail, the interplay of geometry and nature. "My designs are very formal, severe. But walking through my gardens, you always discover fresh surprises, as if the trees are dancing."

ABOVE
"Walking through my gardens," says Caruncho, "you always discover fresh surprises." At S'Agaró, slabs of rough volcanic stone offer a symbolic climb to the terrace above and a view of the Mediterranean.

OVERLEAF
Beauty through a return to utility is the theme at Mas des Voltes, where Caruncho surrounded a foursquare of pools with blocks of grapevines, olive trees, and cypresses in an elegant water garden.

By lengthening the interval between trees in this cypress allée at Mas Floris, Caruncho transformed the double wall of green into a procession of individuals—"monks marching into the woods," as he describes the result.

ABOVE
*Ivy-covered trellises, in the form of liv-
ing walls, enclose a pavilion at S'Agaró,
a shaded, comfortably furnished open-
air living room from which to savor the
spectacle of sun-drenched lily pools.*

LEFT
*The water lily flowers open only at
noon in the pools of S'Agaró; at
other times it is the flashing koi that
provide color and movement.*

LEFT
Gnarled olive trees in this central allée at Mas des Voltes give Caruncho's parterre of wheat, his agricultural paradise, an antiquity as impressive as that of any Greek temple.

OVERLEAF
Downhill from the more formal inner core of Mas Floris lies the vast, three-acre field of lavender. Typical of Caruncho, this gesture is at once simple, bold, and intoxicating.

LUDWIG GERNS
Germany

Clients adore Ludwig Gerns, that's what you hear. When you ask him about this, Gerns laughs. Yes, the German landscape architect says, they typically become "big friends"; each job begins a relationship that carries on long after the final stone is cut and set, the stainless steel polished, the last hedge planted. Such amity confounds the stereotype, for in his design, Gerns is a classicist, and that is a style popularly associated with grandeur and austerity. Yet for Gerns, a garden begins and ends with the people. His is a classicism that is elegant but also warm. His work is precise, but also playful and intimate.

The impulse toward a reconciliation of apparent opposites—of intimacy and warmth with a formal vocabulary—seems to have been with Gerns from the very beginning of his career. He cites two masters as his early inspirations: the lyrical and intensely personal Roberto Burle Marx, and Russell Page, who, though highly innovative, was also self-consciously working within a formal European tradition. But Gerns says that he has since defined his own "way," and indeed what he is doing today is distinctly original.

Gerns's commissions have come from the European heartland of Germany, Switzerland, and Austria. This is a wealthy but also densely populated area where land is expensive and gardens are correspondingly compact. Gerns has found the classical vernacular to be useful for making limited spaces feel expansive. The walls and clipped evergreens that he uses to define space in the classical tradition are also effective in masking limits.

Run a hedge along a boundary, for example, then insert a gate

In a Hannover garden, Ludwig Gerns combines traditional cone-shaped yews with modern elements like this splashing fountain and quiet pool clad in rusted Corten steel. A door-sized "mirror" of reflective metal peeks out of the garden's back hedge.

ABOVE

Near Hannover, an angled wooden footbridge leads over a water basin planted with calla lilies to a sun terrace near the swimming pool.

OPPOSITE

The modernity of this steel-edged pool of water lilies in northern Germany is softened by plantings of 'Kermesina' azaleas and flowering rush (Butomus umbellatus).

or the suggestion of a path, and the visitors' assumption is that the open-air room in which they find themselves is one of a succession. Restrict access to a view and you control the perception of what lies outside the garden. Don't screen a view out, Gerns suggests, but instead allow a calculated glimpse, a tease that sharpens the appetite for more.

Not only is the landscape in which he works congested, but his clients' lives are correspondingly harried. Their gardens are sanctuaries, serene places where the owners can relax. The harmony and order of the classical style is ideally suited to that end. Gerns deliberately avoids including very much floral color—the English-style flower garden, ablaze with bloom, is, to his eye, too aggressive. Instead, he limits the bloom at any given time to a few carefully disposed touches: "It's like the lady has a black blouse and only one diamond on it. It looks more elegant." But, in a calculated progression, as those first flowers fade away, others elsewhere in the garden come into bloom. By changing the blooming focal points, Gerns ensures that the garden recomposes itself throughout the growing season.

Such an emphasis on simplicity and order could be oppressive, since serenity can easily become boring. This danger is avoided by the "tease," the playfulness in Gerns's design. It emerges not only in the tricks he plays with the view, but even more clearly in the way he uses the traditional elements of the classical landscape.

There are, for example, the clipped evergreens that Gerns

"I think it is not a bad idea to do the traditional things, but we live now, and so you have to think about what we do now."

—LUDWIG GERNS

shapes into what he calls "cloud-pruned" topiaries: ascending puffs of greenery held together by gracefully curved trunks and limbs. Gerns often employs the axial layout of the classical tradition, but he typically rotates the terrace at the end of a walk, or sets the focal point at the end of a vista just off to one side. Gerns creates the expectation of symmetry and then provides something else, an element of surprise, a hint of visual tension. Though he typically composes in finely drawn geometrical patterns, his is not the geometry found in traditional formal design.

Instead of running a single path between two points, Gerns is likely to make two paths intersect, paving each with a different stone to create a rhythmic pattern of angles at their meeting point. Even classicists, Gerns explains, have to adapt to the times. "I think it is not a bad idea to do the traditional things, but we live now, and so you have to think about what we do now." The head gardener at Versailles might accept an unquestioning obedience to the rules, but the rest of us are free to create exceptions.

Gerns differs from many colleagues in that he takes his cues for the garden from the house. He begins, naturally, by assessing the site and its potential, but then he heads indoors to assess the ambience that makes his clients comfortable. The garden, he says, "should be another room of the house," for in this way it can best enhance his clients' daily life. It is appropriate, then, that Gerns should be a master of the materials of the garden's built elements. He speaks with a born craftsman's enthusiasm for various glasses and metals, for the cut and polished stones he brings in from quarries in Italy and Spain. Often he will create a hierarchy of hardscapes to denote the different features' relative importance. A secondary path he may pave only with gravel; you will recognize the main route because he surfaces it with meticulously cut stone pavers.

It is the plants, though, that give a garden its special fascination. As they grow, and sometimes overgrow, they transform the landscape while the house remains a still point. Gerns feels a responsibility to ensure that the changes move in a positive direction. That is why his relationship with clients must remain ongoing—that, he says, and the fact that they are friends.

OPPOSITE

An implied river of water, stone, and boxwood cascades down an azalea-covered hillside, drops over a sandstone wall, and continues as a long carpet of boxwood in this intimate garden in northern Germany.

OVERLEAVES

Pages 84–85: *A footbridge directs a visitor's gaze to the sweeping views of the landscape near Hannover. The curved wall of an outdoor shower is surrounded by clipped boxwood, azalea, and Japanese holly (Ilex crenata).*

Pages 86–87: *The elegant composition of this viewing garden is meant to be appreciated from the balconies of the Dusseldorf town house. Gerns's fine attention to building materials is shown in his use of porphyry bricks and low walls topped with pink Estremoz marble. The sculpture is by German artist Will Brull.*

ABOVE

Forms such as the spiraling wall of this outdoor concrete shower are echoed in the arc of the low sandstone wall near the house.

LEFT

The strict but playful geometry of these curving panels of boxwood and Japanese holly is typical of Gerns's work. Accents of red Azalea ponticum and Japanese maple complete the arrangement.

RIGHT

A freestanding wall frames a view of this Hannover house from its drive-way. A bonsai yew and a cloudlike karikomi-style hedge of boxwood steps up to the edge of the wall.

OVERLEAF

A pool of water lilies is the central focus of the terrace of a garden in northern Germany. A low boxwood frame punctuated with clipped box-wood hemispheres surrounds it.

PART TWO THE NEW TRADITIONALISM

PART TWO INTRODUCTION

I f we want things to stay as they are," Giuseppe di Lampedusa warned, "things will have to change." Taken as a comment on Sicilian history, as the great novelist intended, this is a profoundly cynical remark, one that a certain class of politician loves to quote. But for the tradition-minded gardener, the quote makes good sense. (And, for the record, the aristocratic di Lampedusa knew his roses. Only 'Paul Neyron,' the glorious old hybrid perpetual, could please the hero of his masterpiece *The Leopard*—though a prince, he carried the cuttings back from Paris with his own hands.)

The truth is, when it comes to the gardener's art, there is great comfort and strength in tradition. It offers shared ground, a common memory that makes one gardener's references and gestures intelligible to another. A southerner recognizes in another southerner's yard full of camellias and boxwood an implicit claim to a gracious heritage. For a Floridian to reject exotic coconut palms in favor of native coco-plums (*Chrysobalanus icaco*) is a powerful political statement to the neighborhood.

For the extreme examples of this kind of communication, the gardener has to turn to Asia. In China and Japan, especially, tradition has given a special significance to every species of garden plant.

You rarely see roses, for example, in Chinese gardens; to place such a thorny plant in a garden, the spiritual heart of the household, was to attract dissension to the family. To an educated Japanese, bamboo is not just an outsized grass; rather, it is a symbol of resilience and strength. An evergreen, and hence unchanging, foliage has made the pine a favorite of Zen gardeners, who see it as an embodiment of timelessness. Handed down and embellished from generation to generation, this horticultural vocabulary allows the gardener to speak directly and intimately to the visitor.

American gardeners have never shared any nationwide vernacular of this sort. That is not necessarily bad; in fact, it has given our garden design an extraordinary dynamism. The emphasis on figuring it out for yourself has generated a fascinating kaleidoscope of styles, many hideous but others wonderfully fresh. What traditions we do enjoy are typically imports: English and Italian, commonly in the eastern states, and Japanese in the western states.

Tradition, of course, can be a trap. Yoji Sasaki, one of Japan's leading and most innovative landscape designers, has expressed deeply conflicted feelings on this subject. Practicing in a country whose cultural heritage is so vital, Sasaki cannot ignore the past, and in fact he refers to it often in his design. At the same time, though, he is adamant about maintaining independence, lest the power of convention overwhelm his personal, international vision.

Tradition can become tyrannical. If you ask England's well-known horticulturists what is new and exciting in contemporary English gardening, "Not a thing" will be a frequent, if off the record, response. That answer, of course, is not true, as the English gardens included in this volume prove, but the response is a fair indication of how stuck those gardeners sometimes feel among their herbaceous borders.

"If we want things to stay as they are, things will have to change." For a tradition to remain vital, it must be infused with new

ideas, while still, somehow, keeping touch with its roots. This is not an
easy feat, but it can be done. French designer Louis Benech accomplished it in his sensitive and affectionate updating of the historic
Norman manor house La Valeterie. Benech had the advantage of
being familiar not only with the tradition of Norman gardens but also
with that particular garden and even the former gardener. He was
able to update the planting and clarify the design, and thus enhance
the garden without violating the original spirit.

Often the challenge lies in translating a tradition to a new
land—again a difficult task, but one that by its nature frees the
practitioner. When Penelope Hobhouse was commissioned to create
an English-inspired estate in the northwestern Connecticut hills, she
achieved something with a uniquely transatlantic accent. The clapboard house remained just what it was—historic New England—but
with a less flinty flavor in its lush, uncustomarily formal setting.

ABOVE
*Properly handled, tradition is not
enslavement to the past but a resource
for the present, as Louis Benech
proved in his imaginative update of
the garden at a Norman manor house.*

Less parochial than its models on either side of the Atlantic, this is a cosmopolitan retreat for an international age.

Typically, there is an element of the cargo cult in the adoption of nonnative gardening traditions. We read in an anthropology text about Pacific Islanders building imitation landing strips and warehouses in the belief that the appearance of trade goods must inevitably follow, and shake our heads. But how different is it to surround ourselves with the trappings of another time and place in the hope that by so doing we will recapture that bygone lifestyle as well? The interesting thing is that, in gardening at least, the effort sometimes meets with success.

It was, initially, the architecture of the house—pure Cotswold manor—that prompted Edwina von Gal's Long Island client to pursue the dream of a traditional English garden. With von Gal's help, something very much in the Vita Sackville-West mold was achieved, though in the process the model was simplified somewhat and reinforced with plants more appropriate to a North American climate. As you look at the result, it's hard to imagine that spending time on a daily basis in such graceful open-air rooms would not improve the visitor's quality of life. If cramped, ugly quarters can demean, surely elegant ones can exalt.

There are cases where the tradition seems to choose the gardener. A traditional French garden suited not only the French-inspired house of Deborah Nevins's clients, but also their familial needs. The emphasis on formal walks, terraces, and allées promised easy mobility to a child who relies on a wheelchair and a walker. Nevins's clients wanted a space accessible to all. The adjustments this involved—principally a compression of vistas and distances— give an unusual intimacy to what is often a chilly style.

Choosing a tradition does not have to involve making journeys abroad, however. Even where our history of cultivation is relatively brief, it is possible to identify what is indigenous to the way of

OPPOSITE
The look is English in this garden that designer Edwina von Gal created for a Long Island client, but many of the plants are not, a translation needed to make the garden work.

life and pay tribute to that. Illinois dates its tradition of great design back to Louis Sullivan and Frank Lloyd Wright, not long ago by European (or American Indian) standards, but long enough that the heritage is already endangered. The richness of a tradition, according to the owners of Crab Tree Farm, does not depend on antiquity. Their home, the last working farm on the part of Lake Michigan in Illinois, is the masterwork of architect David Adler. In the house they found one of the most gracious country places in America. By extending the house's proportions into the landscape, and emphasizing the use of native plants, they have created a garden that is stately, perfectly adapted to the site, at once traditional and, in the context of our flashier era, courteously subversive. A metaphor, one could say, for the Midwest in general.

Regional pride, power of communication, aspirations for a different way of life—these are all strong reasons to respect tradition in gardening. But the most basic reason is personal. Tradition helps to shape us, but it also reflects the way in which we have, over generations, found life to be most pleasant, most exciting, or most comforting. In turning back to it, what we rediscover is ourselves.

OPPOSITE
The style of Yoji Sasaki's personal garden outside Osaka owes much to the minimalism he absorbed from his father, a painter. His preference for bamboo speaks eloquently to anyone grounded in the Japanese gardening tradition.

LOUIS BENECH
France

Louis Benech's triumphant renovation of this centuries-old manor might be called a modern-day Norman conquest, not that this was a hostile takeover; far from it. Benech knew this garden of old and had been a friend of his predecessor at the estate, Franz Baechler. "Baechler was a wonderful, sweet gardener," Benech says. "I honor his memory in continuing to build the garden."

Americans like to define themselves as a people of the future, and as such we tend to view tradition as a constraint. Benech's experience at La Valeterie, however, suggests otherwise: originality is largely meaningless without a tradition against which to react. Besides, if you set to work (as Benech did at La Valeterie) with a basic design vocabulary already established, you can concentrate on refinements beyond the reach of the gardener who must invent not just the grammar but also the letters.

The view from the house is one of apple orchards, which lend the estate a peaceful, rural atmosphere. Benech respected this rustic feeling, which coexists with the owners' collection of poultry. (And anyone who has had a free-range chicken visit the garden understands how much restraint is required for that.) The designer chose to work with country plants and simple though subtle forms.

To reconnect the house with the restored *pressoir* (the apple pressing house, an important institution in cider-drinking Normandy), Benech inserted a line of yews, clipped in low squares like a trail of stepping-stones. This motif he continued into the herb garden that adjoins the manor house kitchen, reorganizing the planting

OPPOSITE

A trail of stepping-stonelike yews reconnects manor house with pressoir in Louis Benech's respectful yet imaginative updating of a historic landscape at La Valeterie.

OVERLEAF

Rose-covered arches provide a perfumed and nostalgic entrance to the potager, a decorative kitchen garden in the traditional French style.

there into nine squares. Four of these are green; five Benech has gilded, setting out plants of the expected species, but all of golden-foliaged cultivars. Then he wrapped the whole in a ribbon made of fennel, celeriac, and other edible and medicinal plants.

Benech's greater innovation, however, has been to harness natural springs on the property for the creation of a series of ponds, natural mirrors he uses to reflect and deceive. A simple horseshoe-shaped pond greets visitors at the garden's entrance, capturing and throwing back the sky and clouds. Another pond, rectangular in shape, became a through-the-looking-glass device. Benech realized that when the pond was viewed from one end, a field maple (*Acer campestre*) standing on a bank over the pond's opposite edge was an irresistible focal point. Trading on this, he inserted into the slope below the tree a series of hedges—parallel rows of shrubby golden-leaved dogwoods (*Cornus alba* 'Aurea') clipped to resemble a flight of steps. Framing the base of this living staircase at pond's edge with two more bright-yellow-foliaged trees—the golden-leaved gray alders of the cultivar *Alnus incana* 'Aurea'—he made sure that the eye would not skip straight up to the tree but would instead stop at the foot of his living staircase, then climb step-by-step. These steps appear to be uniform, but in fact Benech used a painter's trompe l'oeil to force their perspective. He reduced their height and width so that they appear to recede into the distance, making the maple in turn appear both larger and more distant than it is, and turning a modest pond into a large canal. But walk to the other side, climb up to view the pond from the foot of the maple, and the illusion is reversed—the perspective is foreshortened so that the pond seems not a rectangle but a square.

Benech has also demonstrated a painter's skill in the subtle way he has applied color to the landscape. In a mixed border, he turns up the heat, juxtaposing dark orange primroses, *Primula japonica* 'Miller's Crimson,' against the yellow of *Primula* x *bullesiana*. He keeps a wet meadow from becoming dank, brightening it with the gleam of yellow mimulus and marsh marigolds. In the kitchen garden, he strikes a cooler note, setting sapphire delphiniums to stand guard over a drift of magenta-flowered alliums. In the true spirit of tradition, Benech doesn't seek to replace what went before. He is content to enhance, to show tradition in a new and sometimes startling light.

OPPOSITE

Pleasures of the eye and of the table unite in the potager, where magenta blossoms of ornamental onions vie for attention with blue delphiniums at the foot of an old pear tree.

An air of formality presides in the herb garden, which Benech organized into nine square plots, and then gilded with a planting of golden-leaved cultivars.

Pages 112–113: *Benech turned natural springs into a series of ponds, including this one at the manor's entrance, a horseshoe-shaped mirror of sky and clouds.*

Pages 114–115: *Posing in front of the pink rose 'Eden,' a cock and hen lend the garden a rural air.*

JOHN AND NEVILLE BRYAN

Illinois

To call this a farm, as the Bryans do, is an impressive bit of understatement. When they bought Crab Tree Farm more than fifteen years ago, it was in part to preserve it as the last working farm on Illinois' Lake Michigan shore. Certainly, as they will point out, the Bryans didn't move here because they needed the space, or because the location was convenient. They didn't and it wasn't. Instead, they came here to live because the husband had long admired the house on the bluff; it was built in 1926 by architect David Adler for Mr. and Mrs. William McCormick Blair. John Bryan judged it to be one of the finest surviving examples of Adler's work, and one of the most gracious country houses in America.

In acting on both of these judgments, Bryan showed that his fine eye is backed by considerable imagination. Few shared his enthusiasm for Adler at the time, though he had been Chicago's premier residential architect in his day. Trained at the École des Beaux Arts in Paris, Adler was a master at adapting and combining different historical styles. His genius as a synthesizer, however, was the eventual downfall of his reputation, for the stylistic fluency that made him the darling of North Shore society in the 1920s and 1930s was viewed as backward and derivative by the succeeding generation of modernist architects. Adler has recently been rescued from obscurity by critics, designers, and architects who have come to appreciate his keen sense of design and proportion, talents that produced homes that were functional as well as elegant.

Bryan, however, a businessman with a voracious appetite for the beautiful, understood just what Adler had been after. He liked

OPPOSITE

Mercury and Venus face each other across the walled garden, in John and Neville Bryan's evocation of bygone graciousness.

OVERLEAF

A cello cast in lead leans against a bench, silhouetted against one of the walled garden's Saarinen-inspired windows. John Bryan conceived of this space as an outdoor room.

Bryan limbed up the trees to make dramatic, cathedral-like tunnels, into which the light streams.

the openness of the house; though expansive, it is only one room deep, so that every room has windows on two or three sides. That invites the breezes in during the hot weather, but also makes the house an extrovert. Wherever you stand or sit inside, you are looking at the landscape. The new owner recognized that to really shine, then, the house needed a new setting. He enlisted the help of his wife, Neville.

They were well matched for the renovation. Work takes Bryan to Europe frequently, and he always uses the opportunity to visit galleries, museums, artists, and houses and gardens. Neville Bryan is a tireless dirt gardener, an expert at turning ideas into reality. The couple share a taste for antiques and since the 1960s have amassed one of this country's finest private collections of late-seventeenth- and eighteenth-century English furnishings. The farm was to become the opportunity to display their collection.

But first it was essential to protect the fine period pieces already in residence on the farm. There was the small but exquisite 1920s vintage rose garden, for instance, a rare surviving example of the work of Ellen Biddle Shipman, one of the first women to achieve leadership as a landscape architect. With the help of landscape architect Charles Stick, this garden was refurbished. There was also, at the end of a broad avenue of turf, a pedimented Greek folly, a temple in miniature that was believed to be Adler's work. Bryan left the exterior of it intact, though he converted the interior into a playful homage to Thomas Jefferson, giving it an octagonal floor plan and furnishing it with Monticello reproductions made on the farm. Another Adler gesture was the tennis house. An indoor garden, really, this glass-roofed court had walls wainscoted with topiaried ivy. The Bryans contented themselves with a gentle embellishment, hanging ivy pendants from the roof trusses to provide a festive air for the parties they hold in this space.

The challenge that these disparate elements presented was one of integration. For this to work in the newer, more contemporary features they were planning, the Bryans relied on the farm's natural woodlands. Drawing on what he had studied during trips to England, John Bryan assumed the role, as he says, of "vista cutter." He began to work on a carefully plotted network of connecting paths and allées. Along the edges of these, he limbed up the

OPPOSITE

Semicircular benches offer respite without interrupting the view down Crab Tree Farm's south vista, a grassy avenue connecting house and prairie.

remaining trees to make dramatic, cathedral-like tunnels, into which the light streams on a sunny day.

Bryan connected house and Jefferson folly with a broad, grassy mall; another such avenue, the "south vista," connects the house to a distant prairie. Other features were woven in with smaller walks concealing turns and twists, changing an arrival at the tennis house, the spring garden, or the "English pavilion" into a revelation. Other paths, such as the beach walk and the naturally contoured ravine walk, are experiences in themselves.

While John Bryan edited the woods, Neville Bryan updated the old vegetable garden, turning it into a decorative kitchen garden complete with herb and cutting gardens. She deftly mixed flowers with vegetables, making the whole as attractive as it is appetizing. The work, from starting seedlings in the adjoining greenhouse to expunging weeds from the beds, she does entirely on her own.

Across the way, John Bryan installed a walled garden, an orderly green setting in which to display a prize: an eighteenth-century English reproduction of an ancient Medici Venus. He deliberately designed and finished the space in a 1920s style that Adler himself might have used. One wonders, though, if Adler could have matched the witty placement of another bit of statuary, an eighteenth-century English reproduction of an Italian Renaissance Mercury who stands just outside the gate, forever trying to catch the eye of the goddess within.

Sometimes it is the character of a view or area that dictates the choice of furnishings or ornament. Semicircular benches set face-to-face in the center of the south vista promise repose but, because of their airy design, do not interrupt the sight line. A spot punctuating the way from massive tennis house to horizon-filling lake obviously demanded something strong, so with another flash of humor Bryan installed a statue of Hercules.

The couple's love of England and old-world design permeates every corner of this landscape, and yet, like them, it remains rooted in the Midwest. Close to the house and other architectural areas, Bryan says, you may have "a little pachysandra or hosta," but filling the woods, the farm woods, with such garden-bred plants would be a solecism indeed.

OPPOSITE
The Bryans left the exterior of this 1920s folly intact in the original classical revival style, but converted its interior into an homage to Thomas Jefferson.

ABOVE
Lake Michigan is in view from nearly every one of the house's rooms. Enhancing the sense of place has been the Bryans' consistent priority.

LEFT
A rare example of the work of Ellen Biddle Shipman, this little rose garden was carefully refurbished, the benches rebuilt to Shipman's specifications.

OVERLEAF
This grand, glass-roofed tennis house also serves as a party space today. The ivy pendants are an embellishment of the current owners.

PENELOPE HOBHOUSE
Connecticut

Living in a dream world is something we are all advised against by parents, teachers, therapists, and significant others. The results, though, can actually be quite pleasant, as this garden proves, but only if you have Penelope Hobhouse to guide you through your fantasies.

The grande dame of English garden design, Hobhouse is, as she points out, one-quarter American. That was a crucial credential for this transatlantic project—the client wanted an Edwardian English estate, but he wanted it on the 560 acres he owned in northwestern Connecticut. To take the property back a century in time and across an ocean would seem to require magic, or at least science fiction. But Hobhouse accomplished the translation through simple horticultural know-how and a diplomat's ability to mediate between plants and plan.

Hobhouse has worked on a number of gardens in North America and so came to this project understanding the difficulties of planting English-style in a New England climate. She also recognized that for the illusion to work, she first had to rid the landscape of its rural New England clichés. The main house, a clapboard structure with elements that dated to 1809, was left intact, though its entrance was reframed with shadbushes planted right through the granite cobbles of the front court, and the door was flanked with old English copper washbasins filled with seasonal flowers. But Hobhouse also banished the scribble of pasture fences that crisscrossed the field around the house to create a proper aristocratic sweep. In the process, she repainted the dairy-barn-red

OPPOSITE
Though it may appear like an invitation to a dream, this wooden gate actually provides access to the cutting garden that furnishes flowers, herbs, fruits, and vegetables for the owners' two residences.

> "The contemporary garden is a sort of oasis—a refuge from the pressures of a high-tech, high-speed culture."
>
> —PENELOPE HOBHOUSE

outbuildings a deep, almost black, green with white trim so that they would settle less obtrusively into the vista.

What Hobhouse sought next was not just a Colonial détente but rather, as her associate Nan Sinton explains, a genuine "interaction"—interaction between visitor and garden, of course, but also between American landscape and its English makeover. Her tool for accomplishing this was, on a superficial level, a careful selection of props—architectural follies, pavilions, and pergolas by British architect Sir Anthony Denny, and a small herd of shaggy Scottish Highland cattle. As in any garden, though, the fundamental means of making it all work was the creation of a strong, coordinated structure. In this case, Hobhouse chose to use the geometry characteristic of grand European design, but to simplify and embolden it, giving it a forthright American flavor.

The summit of a nearby hill was an obvious focal point for the view from the house, and Hobhouse enforced this choice by marching a double allée of zelkovas up the slope to the obelisk-crowned folly that she set on the high point. The orchards she planted on either side of the allée continued the sense of geometry, but Hobhouse gave this a jazzier feel by mowing paths on the diagonal through the meadow grass beneath the trees—"a pair of Broadways slicing Manhattan," as one observer described it.

A similar balance was achieved by laying out a formal rectangular garden on either side of the house. The means of enclosure are classically English—on one side, a brick wall, on the other a neatly clipped hornbeam hedge—as are the internal arrangements. Inside the brick wall, you find a kitchen and a cutting garden of square beds framed with brick paths; inside the hedges, a pergola and paired pavilions divide the space into three generous rooms.

Hobhouse's greatest genius, her expressive use of plants, speaks powerfully here. In fact, she speaks in two accents. The tone of the hedged formal garden is pure British understatement, especially in the space closest to the house. This is brilliantly simple, an all-green square punctuated by four saucer magnolias (*Magnolia*

OPPOSITE

A spring display of 'Apeldoorn,' 'General Eisenhower,' and 'Rembrandt' tulips.

OVERLEAF

A decoratively patterned brick path marks the central axis of the walled formal garden; a Kelso bench from Munder Skiles marks its end.

soulangiana) that bury themselves in bloom in May, offering the quieter interest of their smooth gray trunks and branches throughout the rest of the year. Pass through the pergola, and you come into the summer garden, a spectacular arrangement of lush romantic borders that gaze at themselves in the reflective surface of the swimming pool—fringe trees, hydrangeas, roses, and perennials that bloom through the midsummer months. Step a bit farther, between the twinned pavilions, and the seasonal focus changes again, to a fall and spring garden of late flowers such as asters, and shrubs and trees such as viburnums, cotinus, and oxydendrums that offer flowers in the year's early months and bright fruits or changing foliage color in the fall. In winter the architecture of the hedges lends an interest to this garden, and one of the pavilions by this room's entrance has been fitted with a fireplace and a bar to create a comfortable viewing place for the cold months.

In contrast to this succession of subtleties, there is an outspoken quality to the walled cutting and kitchen garden that is more characteristically American. The estate's owner admits to liking large flowers and plants "that capture your imagination." Here, red and yellow dahlias, flame-colored tithonia, blue delphiniums, and violet-red cleomes compete with the outsized, red-green leaves of cannas, all set against a backing of tall perennials, espaliered fruit trees, and climbing roses on the brick walls. Twenty beds marshaled round a central arbor allow plenty of space for herbs and vegetables, too, and every fall the gardening staff plants 1,600 tulips and giant alliums to start off the spring season.

"The garden is evolving," the owner muses. "When I started, the concept was simply to change the look of the place. It has now become a major passion." He takes pride in the estate's self-sufficiency; increasingly, all the food and flowers he and his family use here and in their city residence come from the garden. He has started a nursery, to ensure that understudies of an appropriate size and type will be available should any of the garden trees suffer damage. "The big danger of planting the double allée," Hobhouse observes, "is that its success depends on each tree being perfect."

The owner dreams of reaching back even further into tradition. He's intrigued by the nutteries of eighteenth-century England, collections that the gentlemen farmers of that era assembled of hickories and walnuts and other American trees valued for the harvests of food and timber they provided. Such a scheme cannot be rushed, but with the combination of imagination and practicality already demonstrated here, without doubt it can happen.

OPPOSITE
A rustic Russian house, purchased at an English auction, now sits in a cottage garden all its own, cut out of the surrounding woods.

OVERLEAF
Self-sufficiency is a goal as the garden evolves; the owners relish the superior flavors of homegrown produce.

*The chartreuse of 'Dukat' comple-
ments the intense blues of 'Pacific
Giant' and 'Round Table' delphiniums.*

*A late-summer border in the formal
garden:* Nepeta *'Souvenir d'André
Chaudron,'* Gaura lindheimeri, *and*
Verbena *'Homestead Purple' bloom in
front of white* Hydrangea p. *'Grandi-
flora' and* Phlox *'Mt. Fujiyama,' and
the purples of* Buddleia davidii *and*
Eupatorium *'Atropurpureum.'*

Pages 140–141: *Paired pavilions and,
to the rear, a pergola, all by British
architect Sir Anthony Denny, lend a
decorous English flavor to this Yankee
landscape.*

Pages 142–143: *A gaggle of Chinese
geese steps out across the turf bridge
toward a double allée of zelkovas,
the approach to Sir Anthony Denny's
folly.*

DEBORAH NEVINS
Illinois

There's a special genius to finding new virtues in a centuries-old tradition. That's what Deborah Nevins accomplished in the Francophile landscape she designed for an Illinois family, and the fact that her discovery was to some degree fortuitous in no way diminishes the achievement. Nevins began by listening to the house, but finished by uncovering a potential in French garden design that even the great André Le Nôtre (garden maker to Louis XIV) never realized was there.

Le Nôtre's talent was to fill his clients with a sense of power; his masterpieces, Versailles and Vaux-le-Vicomte, mapped out grand processionals through the surrounding countryside, so that even nature seemed reduced to the status of vassal. Power, however, was not what Nevins's clients wanted so much as empowerment. Their child's mobility was limited by his reliance on a wheelchair or walker, so they wanted a garden that the whole family could enjoy on an equal footing. Such a democratic idea would surely have shocked Le Nôtre. Nevertheless, this couple and their landscape designer found it hidden in his style.

The idea in this Chicago garden is often called "barrier-free gardening." The point is to remove all obstacles that might prevent anyone's enjoyment of the space. This is usually achieved with a retrofit mentality, by the replacement of stairs with ramps and the installation of raised beds to reduce the need for stooping. The results, while well intentioned, typically bespeak the purpose. You recognize a barrier-free garden for what it is at a glance. The Illinois couple wanted something more. In their house, architect

Nevins and her clients wanted a greater intimacy and the sense that wild nature is right at hand.

Thomas Beebe had created a Gallic villa that welcomes everyone, but does so without aesthetic compromises. The clients wanted the same for the grounds.

To ensure that the style of the garden would harmonize with the period of the house, Beebe suggested that the owners work with Nevins, who in addition to her work as a designer is also an architectural historian and a former lecturer on landscape history. The rapport between Nevins and clients was immediate—all three are perfectionists. The mother in particular proceeded to immerse herself in the project, studying books, peppering Nevins with questions, even making trips to France to study the models. It is a testimony to Nevins that she found this client's enthusiasm inspiring rather than exhausting.

Nevins's faith in good design played a major role in making this project work. She did not see accessibility as a challenge. Rather, she maintained that it should be a reflex of good design, like the kick that follows a well-placed tap with the doctor's hammer. It is an article of faith with her that well-articulated spaces encourage intimacy between people and the landscape, and that such intimacy should not be exclusive.

Design began with the organizing of the space near the house, which Nevins, in Le Nôtre's style, laid out much as one would an interior, in a series of clearly defined, rectilinear chambers. The floors of these, and those of the open-air halls that connected them, she chose with care. A mellow Yorkstone had been used in the detailing of the house; Nevins used pavers of this material, both for the sense of connection with the house it gave and for the traction. Set on a bed of stone dust, the Yorkstone slabs provide a firm, flat surface with just enough "tooth" to give a good grip to shoes and rubber tires.

The chambers next to the house were decorated and furnished almost in interior style, with walls of neatly clipped yew, carpets of trim turf, roofs (here and there) of vine-covered arbor. Each space offers a different use or a different experience. There is a topiary garden (a gallery of living art); a lily pond to cool the air on hot

*Yorkstone features in the house's
formal motor court; the entry was set
flush with the ground to simplify
wheelchair access.*

RIGHT

*Banked masses of boxwood embrace
the "amphitheater." Hand-pruning
preserves the box's soft contours.*

days; and the conservatory, a place for sitting rather than for growing plants, through whose transparent walls you can enjoy the garden during unpleasant weather.

The ambience is formal, but not excessively so. The "amphitheater," a sunken semicircular terrace set at one end of the house, is enclosed with a banked mass of box. To encourage compact growth, this is kept clipped, but not sheared—it is painstakingly hand-pruned to preserve the quality of a billowing green cloud bank.

A garden in the Le Nôtre style promotes at least the illusion that the area of control extends to the horizon, or at least as far as the eye can see. Nevins and her clients wanted a greater intimacy with nature. At the edge of the highly structured areas next to the house, Nevins shifted to an unbuttoned style. Paths were kept wide enough to accommodate two people—one in a chair—moving side by side, but the surface became a less formal one of decomposed granite, sprayed with a binder (called Stabilizer) to ensure a nonslip surface. Boundaries and edges, formerly geometric, begin to follow the natural curves and dips of the land. Plantings become less obviously organized. Instead, they tend to extravagant tides and drifts of color, as in the thicket of 'Krinkled White' peonies that form a border in the white garden, or the tapestry of bluebells, hellebores, and miniature narcissi that blooms by an allée of locust trees in spring. This last is emblematic of the designer's compromise between wild and contrived: the tree trunks form a portico of columns to shade the granite path below, but the resulting straight edges are blurred with an underplanting of hostas, astilbes, and ferns.

Farther on, a low-lying area has been enriched with flowering moisture lovers such as Siberian irises to make the "dell." In another area, unclipped evergreens have been brought up next to the path so that the visitor is enveloped in the cool air and scents of a forest—a wilderness experience without the trek.

Comfort and convenience are unobtrusively but attentively addressed throughout this garden. The outer edge of the lawn has been given a sandy subsurface that packs to provide a smooth, hard, fast-draining surface. Similarly, resting places have been provided by the placement of benches and seats along the paths at strategically close intervals. Here, the practical has been successfully crossed with the beautiful to make a place where family members of all ages and conditions meet and reconnect, read, or just enjoy nature on an equal footing. Who cares what the Sun King would have made of this?

OPPOSITE
Around the service court, tulips and crab apples bring clouds of spring color.

OVERLEAF
In traditional fashion, a fountain marks the main axis from the house, punctuating the view from the surrounding gardens.

ABOVE

Still touched with morning dew,
Siberian iris luxuriate in the moist
soil alongside the path to the Dell.

RIGHT

Hostas, astilbes, and ferns soften
the hard edges of the path that runs
through the honey locust allée.

OVERLEAF

An early spring show of bluebells,
hellebores, and miniature narcissus
blooms beneath the allée of honey
locust trees.

ABOVE
*Sedums and spiraea bloom in
the euphorbia garden, one of fifteen
garden rooms.*

RIGHT
*Traditional cottage garden flowers—
hollyhocks, sedum, and cleome—
provide an appropriate setting for
the Cotswold-style guest cottage.*

EDWINA VON GAL

New York

The garden is where we go to relax, so "you can't just be wowed by the beauty of the plants," says landscape designer Edwina von Gal. "You need to offer a more disciplined view." It was the search for this antithesis, for a reconciliation of sensual and rational pleasures, that brought von Gal this Long Island client. An accomplished photographer with a background in art history, the client had tried several times to begin a garden, but never achieved anything that satisfied her. The architecture of the house, a Cotswold-style manor house with a Cotswold cottage guesthouse, had suggested an English garden. The owner studied books and magazines and made pilgrimages to England, where in the genuine Cotswolds she was bowled over by an early 20th-century masterpiece, Lawrence Johnston's Hidcote Manor. Vita Sackville-West's famous garden at Sissinghurst Castle in Kent (inspired, in part, by Johnston's achievement) also impressed her deeply, as did Westwell, Anthea Gibson's garden in Burford, Oxfordshire. In all of these it was the sweet and sour contrast, the sensuality of the plantings within a strictly formal structure, that impressed her.

She understood what she wanted, but not how to achieve it. For that, the owner turned to von Gal. The two set to work building the garden as they would a house, with von Gal as architect and the owner as the decorator.

Following the pattern the owner had admired in the English gardens, von Gal decided to treat the space architecturally, dividing it with head-high hedges into the series of discrete spaces, or

OPPOSITE

Through the garden gate, past the embrace of purple-flowered buddleias, the visitor steps from Long Island into a personal Cotswold hideaway.

> "You can't just be wowed by the beauty of the plants, you need to offer a more disciplined view."
>
> —EDWINA VON GAL

"rooms." This approach has the advantage of seeming to increase a property's space. Because you experience the area only gradually, in a series of discoveries, it feels much larger than it does if left open, a blank lawn captured in a glance. Dividing the area into rooms lets the gardener serve up a series of different experiences, a succession of courses, rather than presenting the visitor with just one big dish.

There is a danger in this treatment: if you break up the experience, a single garden can become many unrelated ones. Unless a sense of coherent progress is maintained, some sort of map built in to pull the visitor through from one area to another, the whole is likely to degenerate into a chaotic series of disjointed and clashing impressions. To avoid this, von Gal arranged the rooms, fifteen in all, along a backbone of paths, a broad main axis that runs straight back from the rear of the house, crossed at intervals by smaller secondary walks. To give these lines greater presence, von Gal edged them with additional hedges or ran them through allées of compact trees selected to suit the scale of the space. Lindens are the tree of choice for this purpose on the estates of England, but avenues of trees so large would only emphasize the more modest size of this property. The handsome but smaller pears and hawthorns von Gal used had the effect of expanding the apparent size of the property.

Von Gal made another substitution in the shrub she selected for the hedges. The English choice for this purpose has been, traditionally, the yew. This can make a handsome, needled wall, but it is vulnerable to winter kill in the harsher North American climate, and its slow rate of growth is unsuited to the get-it-done-today American schedule. That is not a problem with the fast-growing privet from which von Gal made her hedges, and it's among the hardiest of shrubs, almost unkillable.

There is a room and an experience to suit almost any mood here. To entertain in style, you can take your cocktails out into the polished parterre, a quartet of low hedge embroideries next to the house; for a more intimate meeting, you can step over into a cozy little euphorbia garden, with its tousled mix of shrubs and perennials spilling out of their beds to embrace the jigsaw paving of irregular

OPPOSITE
The shrub rose 'Seafoam' drops a summertime flurry of snow-white petals onto a bluestone terrace.

*Sedums and spiraea bloom in
the euphorbia garden, one of fifteen
garden rooms.*

*Traditional cottage garden flowers—
hollyhocks, sedum, and cleome—
provide an appropriate setting for
the Cotswold-style guest cottage.*

flagstones. Two-tone hedges circumscribe the pear allée, a place of ceremonious order, while a fertile profusion of flowers and foliage characterizes the garden room fronting the cottage at one end of the great lawn.

If hedges provide the punctuation that divides these spaces, it is the ornaments the owner has chosen that link one to the other, continually drawing you in and on. Look down the main axis from the house, and a large Grecian urn at the far end supplies the vista's focal point. Walk down to inspect that and your eye is caught along the way by terra-cotta pots, a large Deco statue of the goddess Diana, a birdbath, a fountain and sundial, a wrought-iron bench, a topiaried dwarf spruce rising out of a potbellied container, and, near the cottage, a woven-straw beehive.

The owner and von Gal understand the power of a system, but they also recognize the benefits of occasionally violating its rules. The perpendicular pattern this garden follows in the relating of one part to another is basic to its aristocratic style. A swimming pool, though, is where you go to relax, and von Gal set this one kitty-corner to the rest of the garden, tucking in behind it a triangle of flowers for cutting, or for admiring as you dry off after your plunge.

Originality supposedly is the art of concealing the sources from which you borrow. In the garden, though, why bother? All gardeners borrow seeds, cuttings, and ideas from one another. If you are borrowing from the best, as the two women of this garden have done, then why hide your debt? Especially if the borrowing is an intelligent reinterpretation. Lawrence Johnston, Vita Sackville-West, and Anthea Gibson would have no trouble finding their way around this Long Island landscape. They would recognize many of its elements. One suspects, though, that they would be surprised at the slightly crisper lines, that they might admire, even envy, the tougher New-World planting—and that, above all, they would welcome the two women not as imitators but as colleagues.

A terra-cotta urn draws the eye and turns the foot past the terraces and parterres, across the great lawn, and through the rose garden to the final hawthorn allée.

Garden ornaments chosen by the owner have been put to work as focal points to punctuate the views and walks and lure the visitor from one space to another.

YOJI SASAKI

Japan

The very strength of the Japanese gardening tradition is what makes it a challenge for Yoji Sasaki. Even today, geographical and political isolation permits a remarkable continuity of cultural development in this island nation, despite the shocks and stimuli of more recent history. In his work as a landscape architect, Sasaki can draw on what he calls "metaphors" from as long ago as the Heian period (A.D. 784–1185), confident that they will still resonate with his public. Yet, for a designer such as he, with an international perspective and the determination to break new ground, this heritage can also be constraining, something to be kept at arm's length.

Sasaki says that he gave little attention to this aspect of his cultural inheritance until he was studying abroad, first as an undergraduate at the University of California at Berkeley and later at the Harvard School of Design. It was during this time as an outsider that he first thought deeply about the distinctive character of Japanese culture. Through this external prism he began exploring the Japanese design tradition. But, he hastens to add, while doing so he was also pursuing what amounted to an apprenticeship with the eminent American modernist Peter Walker. Indeed, as the son of a minimalist artist, Sasaki was well prepared to absorb Walker's lessons in the power of abstraction and simplicity.

The challenge Sasaki has faced in synthesizing the traditional and the new is, to a degree, that confronted by Japan, a country in love with modernity but also committed to its past. This challenge is what makes Sasaki's work, while cosmopolitan in flavor, so intrinsically Japanese.

OPPOSITE

Two traditions interlace in a path at the Speaker's house. Fingers of Western-style turf reach out between cut-stone pavers to touch those of native Japanese pebble pavement.

Sasaki compares the elements of this garden to actors on a stage: "self conscious in their graceful simplicity, silent between revealing acts."

Nowhere is the tension between old and new more apparent than in the garden he designed for the official residence of the Speaker of Japan's House of Representatives. Completed in 2001, this project was an extraordinary opportunity. With the support of the architect for the house, Shozo Uchii, Sasaki was given a free hand in the surrounding site, 4.7 acres right in Tokyo, 4.7 acres of the most expensive real estate in the world. But with it came a seemingly irreconcilable assignment: he was to make a typically Japanese garden that would accommodate the Speaker's need for entertaining in a Western style.

This conflict encapsulates two very different definitions of what a garden should be. In Japan, it has traditionally been treated as a work of art, something to be savored by viewing from carefully defined vantage points. The contemplative nature of such a composition would seem obviously and utterly incompatible with the contemporary Western understanding of the garden as "activity center," or, as a Californian such as Peter Walker might put it, a place for outdoor living.

Sasaki found a resolution, or at least the clue to one, in the history of the site. It had been the location, he learned, of a Tokugawa period (1603–1867) garden, though that had disappeared under the bulldozers of the U.S. Army, which cleared the land for its own use during the post–World War II occupation. Sasaki found only a heap of broken stones and the indistinct remnant of a pond when he first visited. Those scraps, however, suggested a solution to him.

He turned for inspiration first to a painted screen of Tokugawa artist Yu-syo Kaihoku, a seaside landscape painted for the imperial family in the sixteenth century; in this he found the calm and grace that would become the keynotes for the Speaker's garden. He restored the pond, using the salvaged stones, to a style typical of that period's Edo school of design. To make this work with a modern house and the landscape's modern elements, Sasaki went back even farther, taking a "metaphor" from a typically Heian garden plan, that of a house or palace connected to a pond by a corridor and a "fishing pavilion."

To one unschooled in the Japanese garden tradition, though, what Sasaki created here looks suspiciously like something that

might appeal to a minimalist artist like his father. The corridor in his version is reduced to a suggestion of a path. Directed along the axis of the house, it is an austerely eloquent track of gray cut-stone slabs set on edge and parallel as neat as a swatch of corduroy. Starting at the door, this masonry strides straight down to and into the pond.

Besides uniting house and water, this path is also divided—one side is an expanse of turf, a very un-Japanese feature to be used for the lawn parties essential to the Speaker's entertaining. Directly opposite is Sasaki's interpretation of a moss and sand garden, a traditional Japanese garden form that he has reduced almost to an abstraction. You can imagine it pleasing equally a modernist colleague and a Zen monk.

Reduction is, in fact, a central part of Sasaki's design style. "Not busy" but "quiet" is his goal. The Japanese gardener has traditionally copied from nature; Sasaki reduces naturalism to abstraction.

A case in point is the garden he created around his own home—Hakuu-kan ("white rain house")—just outside Osaka. The place is

ABOVE

Spare elegance is the keynote at Sasaki's own "white rain house" (Hakuu-kan), where the landscape architect has pursued "a dialogue of light and shadows."

a complex of structures, including a house for his immediate family, a studio for his father, separate units for his children, and rental studio lofts. The garden space, which begins with the courtyard in front of the entrance to the main house and adjoins the parking area next to the street, is small, approximately 150 square meters in all, but it seems spacious; starkly simple, yet subtly complex.

The intent, according to Sasaki, was to bring nature to the forefront of the residents' daily life. He did this through the calculated manipulation of what he calls ephemeral elements—light, shadow, and wind—which by their constant change call attention to the progress of the day itself and of the seasons. He accomplished this with the interplay between the built elements, principally stone, concrete, and glass, and the simple plantings. What could have seemed sparse—a few stalks of bamboo framed by an opening in a fence, a recumbent maple rising from behind a bed of horsetails—took on dignity and power from careful placement. The beauty inherent in uncomplicated plants becomes apparent when they are treated respectfully. Sasaki compares the elements of this garden to actors on a stage, "self-conscious in their graceful simplicity, silent between revealing acts."

As important as the actors is the set, and in this, too, Sasaki worked with a seeming artlessness that is actually anything but. A canvas on the street side filters the view, casting a changing pattern of shade that Sasaki describes as "a dialogue of light and shadows." Clean white walls become the screen on which various garden elements are projected as the sun moves across the sky. At night, artificial lights stain these surfaces with different patterns. Like the courtyard, these garden effects work into the house's interior. The raindrops that collect on one skylight at night, Sasaki notes, project a superb pattern the next morning on the living room wall as they intercept the sun. He likens this effect to Chinese calligraphy; it was for this his elder brother, a poet, named the family home Hakuu-kan.

The sensitivity to detail and the ability to find the greater beauty in small things are what place this very modern designer so firmly in the Japanese tradition. Could a Western designer create calligraphy from raindrops? Perhaps, but who would notice it in our rush to fill our gardens with activity? That, finally, seems to be the essential point Yoji Sasaki found in the Japanese garden heritage: the understanding that the garden should encourage meditation, stillness. "Not busy" but "quiet." Only an unconventional man, a native with the outsider's perspective, could reinterpret the tradition so well.

OPPOSITE
An extension of the central hall of the Speaker's house, the garden's principal path divides two experiences—to the right, a lawn for Western-style entertaining; to the left, a garden, inspired by the Japanese tradition, for quiet thought.

ABOVE
*Entry to Sasaki's Hakuu-kan is made
through an austere glass-enclosed
foyer, minimally ornamented with
horsetails (front) and a single bowed
maple.*

OPPOSITE
*The transparent walls of the foyer
bring the garden right into the house.
Every object outside is as carefully
chosen and placed as those inside.*

The view from the Speaker's house encompasses a garden that has roots in Japan's garden tradition but a stripped-down character that Sasaki absorbed from his father's minimalist paintings.

OVERLEAF

Sasaki's design for the Speaker's house marries not only East and West but also present and past—an achievement possible only for the native with an outsider's perspective.

PART THREE THE NEW
NATURALISM

FEATURED DESIGNERS
IN THIS SECTION:

ALAIN IDOUX
France

PATRICK CHASSÉ
New York

WILLIAM PETERS
Idaho

STEVE MARTINO
Arizona

DAN PEARSON
England

PART THREE INTRODUCTION

For gardeners, the relationship with nature has always been complicated. We may court nature, and say that we wish to take it as our partner in the garden, but the unspoken truth is that we want the partnership to be on our terms. Today, some of us no longer seek to conquer nature, as our ancestors did; with our better grasp of ecology, we may prefer to woo it. We may profess an honest love of nature, but it is an imperfect kind of love, the slightly adolescent sort that believes the beloved is perfect—or will be, just as soon as we have taught him or her to dress and behave appropriately. The fundamental impulse of gardening is the idea that we can improve on whatever it is we have been given.

After all, if we really wanted our gardens to be natural places, we would not garden at all. We would keep our hands in our pockets, let the weeds have their way, and see what develops.

Fortunately, there is a compromise. It's called naturalism, which, despite the name, is not natural, or at least not simplemindedly so. Naturalism is the gardener's interpretation of nature, an attempt to extract the themes and principles from the details of what you see—and then work with them.

On a practical plane, this is what every skillful gardener does. We have learned to mulch from plants that cover the ground with organic litter that keeps the soil around them moist and cool while repressing the germination of competitive weeds. We plant for diversity not only to gratify our acquisitive instincts but also because we have learned that botanical diversity gives the garden greater resilience when challenged by pests and diseases.

The naturalist, though, elevates designing with nature from an expedient to an aesthetic. He bases the themes as well as the details of the design on a close reading of nature in its local incarnation. Dan Pearson, a current leader of England's naturalistic garden designers, takes direction from what he finds on a site. "The landscape," he has said, "tells you which way the wind comes from, what the soil is like, and what those conditions are doing to the plants." After he has gathered these clues, though, what Pearson develops from them is not a reproduction, but an interpretation.

Or, as a client said of the naturalistic garden Patrick Chassé created for him in the hinterlands of Westchester County, "We just took what the glacier did, and made it better."

And though it may be hubris to say so, he is right, at least from the perspective of beauty, comfort, and utility, as well as from that of most wildlife, which finds the botanically enriched, varied habitat of Chassé's sensitively naturalistic landscape more attractive than he sometimes might wish. Not that a naturalistic garden is in any sense a replacement for true wilderness. Yet as the point of intersection between nature and the human landscape, the naturalistic garden has a special fascination.

That is in part because it is one of the most difficult styles of design to master. To succeed, the garden must be a duet, with the designer playing in close harmony with nature. Counterpoint, however, is also important; the confrontation between man and nature works like a spice. The late Alain Idoux, a sculptor by training,

liked to place regionally appropriate artifacts—an ancient Roman column, perhaps—in the midst of his stark, Provençal vistas. Steve Martino builds the contrast into his work by his choice of locales—though in love with the desert, he designs in Phoenix for urban clients and has described his art as one of "bringing the desert into the city."

In part, this confrontation is a trick. Leading viewers to identify one part of the garden or, as in Martino's case, the setting. as obviously artificial creates a supposition that the rest is not. Reinforcing that impression demands a high degree of craft: the naturalistic designer must be expert at covering his tracks. The evidence of manipulation should not intrude. Pearson prefers his gardens to be maintained just at the edge of neglect, so that they develop a patina of wildness.

ABOVE
"We just took what the glacier did and made it better," the client said of this magical scene by Patrick Chassé.

A trademark planting of acacia, prickly pear, ocotillo, and saguaro by Phoenix-based landscape architect Steve Martino.

This deception is, generally, unconscious: The designer would say he simply prefers the unstudied look. The audience is his willing accomplice. It is the impression that the garden was not constructed—that it just happened—that gives it its impact. A stroll through a meadow or grove should leave the visitor marveling at nature's wonders, not admiring the gardener's ingenuity. Disneyland is lots of fun, but it's Yosemite (and as a park, this too is a planned landscape) that makes you feel close to something larger than yourself. Naturalistic design is, in this sense, a selfless endeavor.

And yet, at its most successful, this sort of design can put its creator in the godlike position of dictating to nature on a grand scale. Trees don't gather naturally in clumps on hilltops, where Lancelot

"Capability" Brown, the leading landscape designer of eighteenth-century England, put them to enhance the topography of his clients' estates. Nor do all natural contours follow the "line of beauty" (not too much curve, not too little—just enough) that Brown favored. So majestic was the effect of Brown's design, however, that admirers insisted it was simply an expression of nature's best.

A rapidly proliferating best it was. Over the course of his career, Brown reshaped more than 150 of England's grandest estates, many of which ran to thousands of acres. As he did so, his vision of nature became something akin to the national norm. Horace Walpole, aristocratic tastemaker of the day, put the matter neatly in a letter he wrote to a gardening friend at the time of Brown's death: "Your Dryads must go into black gloves, Madam. Their father-in-law, Lady Nature's second husband, is dead!" Brown's influence lived on, though, so imbedded in the popular perception of what southern England ought to look like that after two and a half centuries of grooming and "restoration" the countryside has largely come to fit Brown's aesthetic. Nature, in short, has shown what that designer liked to call "capabilities for improvement."

This is not an isolated case. Frederick Law Olmsted had a comparable impact on the imagination of nineteenth-century America, and the Midwest still, in large measure, defines its prairie-scape according to the ideas that Jens Jensen brought with him to Chicago as a 24-year-old immigrant from Denmark. Will Steve Martino play the same Pygmalion role in the Southwest? And no one who views the sculptural, bare-boned gardens of the late Alain Idoux will ever again see the landscape of Provence in quite the same way. Nature, apparently, found yet another husband in him.

ALAIN IDOUX

France

A vacation in this southern region of France—a week, or even a year, in Provence—is pleasurable, easy. To live here, however, either as a plant or as a gardener, is not. Beautiful this rugged land of mountains, rock, and perennial drought may be, but growing anything in the thin, dry soil is a challenge. As Alain Idoux proved, however, the rewards for persistence can be magnificent.

Idoux, who died of Lou Gehrig's disease in 1999 at age forty-six, was a native of Provence, as at home there as the aromatic herbs that clothe its hillsides. His vision, though, was not at all parochial. In his twenties he had gone to Israel, first to study sculpture and then to teach it, and had fallen in love with the asceticism of the desert. He returned to France to exhibit his work in Paris and afterward stayed on to teach in Normandy, where he found himself increasingly drawn to working with the land. This new passion drew him back to the material he knew best, the landscape that he still found most intriguing and most challenging. He moved back to Provence.

The move paid off, for stubborn as this land can seem, Idoux understood it thoroughly. The gardens he made not only look at home, they flourish with almost no irrigation. What another designer might have perceived as hostile or unkempt in the rough terrain, Idoux recognized as vigorous and beautiful. The more ascetic the site, the more enthusiastic Idoux's response. His standard opening gambit in making a garden was not to clear away stone. Rather, after clearing away weeds so that he could read the

OPPOSITE

Water is the most precious gift in the arid south of France; Idoux created this rill from old roof tiles and framed it with honeysuckle and rows of young fruit trees.

land and identify valuable trees, he brought in more stone. Idoux would select stones that pleased him, such as the old milestone he chose for a garden in the Alpilles Mountains, and set them up on the site like sculptures. Then he would move them around, using them to mark and to draw the eye to different perspectives.

Idoux's approach to garden-making always remained that of the artist rather than of the architect or engineer. He would take photographs, then piece them together to fashion a panoramic view of a site, then overlay this with tracing paper and begin to sketch with pastels.

This approach perfectly suited his clients in the Alpilles, who were collectors of contemporary art and wanted an outdoors to complement the works they had assembled inside. What Idoux eventually presented to them was a series of terraces, clean of line, surfaced with limestone and gravel—and, in a compromise with the owners ("the only compromise," they have said), a few panels of turf. To bound and define the terraces he piled up low dry-stone walls, planting into the crevices indigenous herbs such as teucrium, myrtle, and rosemary. Just beyond, he planted a *jardin de senteurs*.

A garden of scents, that is. Provence is the home of the French perfume industry, and fields of lavender cover the countryside. Like Idoux, lavender is native to the region, and he adopted it, planting it not in a farmer's parallel rows but instead in a purple-blossomed, silver-leaved star shape that draws the eye and then sends it out to the distant, jagged peaks.

At the other side of the house, a stepped path makes its way through sweeps of ornamental grasses, through an allée of olives ringed with santolina to a secret garden shaded by an ancient walnut. Farther out, he found another aged tree, a gnarled almond standing alone in the wild grasses. This became another focus; Idoux spiraled out from it a band of white limestone punctuated at regular intervals with younger almonds—a dance of the trees, from which a narrow path leads through a screen of wild boxwood to a barren spot that Idoux deliberately made more barren. With a high-pressure jet of water, he scoured away the soil to expose the rock ledges, then inserted into them circles of desert plants.

Idoux was not interested in drought-tolerant gardens. He had the imagination to embrace the local climate and make its challenge the garden's strength. However, a commission to make a garden for a small château at the foot of Mount Ventoux demanded something grander, and on a slope below the residence, he created a dry torrent of stones. The concept is not new—the dry creek bed,

"Stones are civilized. Stones make a garden."

—ALAN IDOUX

or wash, has become a standard feature of hillside gardens in the American Southwest—but Idoux's genius gave this conceit a twist that made it fresh. The usual approach is the literal-minded one of lining the channel with water-rounded river rocks and pebbles. Idoux, instead, collected jagged limestone slabs, setting them on edge to fashion a tumbling, kinetic torrent. You can't help yourself: You sniff for the spray, listen for the roar.

Above, on a series of terraces stepping up to the château, Idoux used stones differently yet again. These are worked stones, architectural fragments that Idoux rescued to tame the landscape. Behind the château he discovered a broken Roman column, and he set this at the end of the terrace, to make a focal point. On the terrace below he erected a seventeenth-century facade that he had found lying on the ground at a local stone yard. Not far from the château entrance, to mark the entry to the garden, stands the ghost of an old arch. Someday, the allée of almond and fruit trees he planted will furnish a stately approach. In the meantime, a rill of springwater runs down a channel of old roof tiles to entice visitors.

Vegetation judiciously applied softens what might otherwise be too much hardscape. Solemn cypresses echo the fractured column on the upper terrace, framing views, while perennials and shrubs add serene hues of yellow, blue, and white. You step into another mood when you enter the strong architectural setting of the lower terrace with its pool. The planting here is of fruitfulness: of lemons and oranges in terra-cotta pots and the bold, vigorous oranges and golds of trumpet vine, heleniums, heliopsis, and potentillas. Step down one more level and you disappear into a labyrinth of clipped yew and santolina.

The ample greenery is enough to keep a horticulturist busy. Nevertheless, you cannot help feeling that Idoux preferred to express himself with the stones. That was partly the sculptor in him, but also something more. Underlying the love of the wild, of romance and metaphor, there was in Idoux a Provençal, peasant thrift: "When you have a small budget and a big landscape," he explained, "it is better to adapt the vegetation and then punctuate the space with stones."

OPPOSITE

At a château near Mount Ventoux, Idoux set up this fragment of an ancient Roman column, then surrounded it with dark cypresses, boxwood, and pale flowers.

ABOVE
*Regal lilies look startlingly fresh
against a blue Provençal sky, their
delicacy a counterpoint to the rugged
terrain.*

RIGHT
*Rather than clearing stones from the
landscape, Idoux usually imported
more, as in the Alpilles garden, where
he spiraled a band of white limestone
out from an aged almond tree.*

OVERLEAF
*Setting jagged limestone slabs on
edge, Idoux created a torrent of stones
rushing down the hill from the Mount
Ventoux château.*

PATRICK CHASSÉ
New York

For Patrick Chassé, as for Alain Idoux, a garden begins with the stone. He loves and knows plants intimately. He understands the power of water, too, and uses it with skill. But rock, that is the garden's most enduring element. It shapes the land, sets the tone. Chassé understands this and treasures the stones accordingly. If they unearth a rock, most gardeners hasten to remove it. Chassé is more likely to remove the soil, better to expose his find.

In this respect, Chassé was the obvious choice to design a garden in Westchester County. The site was ideally suited to his talents. Thirty-odd miles from New York City, with a lake, a brook, and, above all, a wealth of glacial rock, this site was a gem and Chassé the man to set and polish it.

Fortunately, the owners were collaborators after Chassé's own heart. The husband, whose Manhattan gallery deals in ancient and medieval art, has a well-developed sense of color, form, and style. He also knows the importance of proper placement and display; indeed, he's proven as tireless as Chassé in seeking out the right element for each spot, and the right spot for each element. For this garden, a state of flux is the constant. "Nothing is safe here," the owner cheerfully observes.

Placement began with the movement of the boulders that an ancient ice sheet had deposited on the site thousands of years earlier. Then Chassé played glacier himself, trucking in more rock and artfully spilling this down the slope to form a path from the house toward the landscape below. With a characteristic touch of whimsy, he replaced the pool's diving board with a boulder, and tumbled

OPPOSITE

Chassé carpeted this grove of paper birches, visible from the house, with cinnamon fern and blue-leaved hostas for a lush woodland effect.

The entire stock of a failing nursery's
tree peonies was brought in to bank
the house with outsized blossoms.

OPPOSITE
Set in a treetop, the glass-enclosed
crow's nest furnishes a bird's-eye view
of landscape and lake.

more boulders around the pool's edge before the surrounding pavement was set. Chassé wanted to preserve the impression that
nature, not man, was in control.

This attitude is central to Chassé's work as a designer, for it
bespeaks not only an emotional conviction but also, it seems, an
intellectual one. Chassé's education was, for an artist, an exceptional one. As a teenager, he had been captivated by his accidental
discovery of an extraordinary garden near his home on Mount
Desert Island in Maine. While hiking through the woods, he'd come
across an open gate and had stolen in to find himself in what he
later learned was a gift to the public, the former garden of local
artist Charles Savage. Savage had been a disciple of Beatrix Far-
rand, America's first great female landscape architect and the
designer of many of Mount Desert's showplace estates.

Chassé was deeply impressed by what he saw in the Savage
garden. Many years later, he was to restore its plantings, and he
still takes clients there to show them the magnificent rock ledges.

ABOVE
A pond-side pavilion, draped in wisteria, offers a shaded viewing plat-form in summertime and, in good weather, the spot for a scenic lunch.

But when it came to a choice of professions, it seemed at first that Chassé was going to study nature through a microscope. He was well on his way to a degree in biology at the University of Maine, spending summers in a cancer lab near home, when he was drafted by an acquaintance to help identify ferns she was collecting for her garden. Lured once again into the field, Chassé discovered that for him there was no going back. He ended up pursuing a degree in landscape architecture at Harvard, so that he could interpret nature rather than merely study it.

Chassé's rare combination of emotional involvement and scientific discipline makes his design not only appealing but also authentic. That is apparent in his work with the rocks in the Westchester County garden, and with the plants there as well. The planting of the garden, a process in which the husband actively participated, was, like the stonework, a coordination of human needs with natural imperatives. It also reflects an artist's need to arrange and heighten experience. On one level, Chassé wrote a story here with the greenery, a mystery, a horticultural thriller.

As he found it, the landscape was too obvious; the lawn and tennis court below the house and the lake below that were open to view. "When we came here it was like looking down at a landing field," the owner recalled. The new planting changed that. Shrubs and trees were introduced to interrupt the vista, define different areas, and turn a garden walk into an extended exploration.

But it was also, to be honest, a case of plants for plants' sake. The owner proved to have as lively an appreciation for masterpieces of this sort as for those he handled in his gallery. But it was Chassé, he explains, who was his teacher. "Patrick taught me to notice different foliage colors and textures." The owner has learned to admire the way the mist of a purplish-brown fennel contrasts with the broad plates of a blue-green hosta, the richness of a fern's green fronds against the chalk-white bark of paper birch. A once barren slope became a cascade of mountain laurel after they bought out the stock of a nursery that was going out of business. From another failing grower, they bought every tree peony he had, so that more than a hundred now flourish in a billow of bloom to the northeast of the house. The owner fell in love with the graceful shape and structure of weeping trees, and Chassé worked into his design weeping beeches, birches, willows, styraxes, and katsuras.

Yet not all the gestures are bold. The owner, having lost his taste for bright colors, is banishing the more brilliantly hued azaleas. He won't tolerate the acid-yellow daylilies, only those with creamy blossoms. You have to hunt among the rocks to find the collection of hellebores, and here and there in shady corners for the epimediums. What's most remarkable is the way in which the exotic and the choice are married with native woodland plants and then fitted in among the rocks—the naturalistic garden at its best.

The reason it all works, no doubt, is the dreamy sense of magic the garden has taken on—the feeling that here anything is possible. This is most intense by the pond that Chassé excavated between the tennis court and the lake. A wisteria-draped pavilion sits on the bank, offering a place to rest and, on fine days, a place for lunch. You can also wander out over the water on the Japanese-inspired zigzagged bridge of planks. This takes you deep into the parasol-sized leaves of the lotus, where pink flowers are as big as bowls and where the soberest adult cannot help but feel a child again.

Or, if you will, you can rise above it all, soar like a bird. Follow yet another stone path from the house's back door, continue off the crest of the hill on another plank bridge, and you suddenly find yourself among the treetops. The round viewing platform, enclosed only by a curved sheet of transparent glass, seems to float in midair. So, too, do you—omnipotent for the moment or, at least, omniscient.

ABOVE
Water droplets sparkle on a giant,
blue-green lotus leaf that rises like
a parasol above the pond's mirrored
surface.

RIGHT
A Japanese-inspired bridge zigzags
through plants, meandering out
across the water.

OVERLEAF
Having lost his taste for bright colors,
the garden's owner, with Chassé's
help, is indulging in softer composi-
tions such as this tousle of Russian
sage, Japanese blood grass, miscan-
thus, and fountain grass.

WILLIAM PETERS

Idaho

I t is an American dream and, usually, an American tragedy. You find a place of extraordinary natural beauty, and it's for sale. You buy it, create a home there, and in domesticating the landscape you destroy precisely that which attracted you. "Gardeners," William Peters explains, "typically impose."

But not always, and the garden that Peters, a California-based landscape architect, created in partnership with two clients in Sun Valley, Idaho, is proof of that. In its lighter touch, this garden presents a model for something new. It also marks a coming-of-age for the American gardener, a move away from Old-World concepts.

All three creators habitually use the word "we" when speaking of this garden; unlike most architect/client relationships, the one between William Peters and the garden's owners—a retired couple from Michigan—has been a true partnership. For fifteen years they worked together in what Peters calls a dialogue with nature. The three put a great deal of themselves into this Idaho mountainside. Yet the changes they made were so carefully attuned to the spirit of the place that a first-time visitor wonders where the garden is. Gradually, however, you are drawn into an experience that is subtle but deep, a piquant alternation of serenity and surprise.

This garden began with the owners' love of Sun Valley's special character. The husband was a Yale undergraduate in 1942, when he first visited the area, and he treasures the memory of the rebuke that his reckless skiing earned him from the movie star Claudette Colbert. He brought his wife to the valley twenty years later, and though she doesn't ski, she loved the peace and the space. Both

Though seemingly untouched, the groves of aspens that surround the house were actually planted to define the landscape's spaces and are periodically replaced as they outgrow their spots.

were excited to acquire two acres overlooking the historic Sun Valley Lodge. They were aware that injuries to the hoary sagebrush that carpeted the site would be painfully slow to heal. That's why, when they began building their home in 1975, they enclosed the construction area with a fence and told the workmen that no one was to stray outside the barrier.

Crafted from granite, concrete, and glass, the house has the look of a rocky outcrop. It would not be easy to create a compatible garden. Aside from everything else, the growing season in Sun Valley lasts a mere six weeks. Spring's final frost usually comes at the end of June and there is snow again by the end of August. Above all, the couple wanted to avoid the mistake they saw in the town below, where wealthy immigrants were turning the pristine landscape into an alpine Scarsdale.

They realized they needed special help. When their decorator recommended a landscape architect in Marin County, it did not seem too far to go—especially when, on his first visit to Sun Valley, William Peters told them, "We'll keep it natural." Peters began to commute to Idaho every spring and fall.

The new partners' first act was to soften the architectural edges with clumps of aspens, whose placement is subject to intense debate; each year the partnership must decide on additions and subtractions, and everyone partakes in the pruning.

When the owners decided to add an office wing to the house, the partnership turned this into an opportunity. On the roof, soil was laid down, then planted with fescue. Left shaggy, this further roots the house into the slope.

Placing the owners' artworks has been an ongoing task. A couple of oversized, sinuous stainless-steel pieces by the Israeli-born sculptor Gidon Graetz fit particularly well. They are set on swiveling bases, so that every side can be viewed from the house and garden, and their gleaming metal picks up, bends, and reflects the surroundings. Peters placed a pair of cut-granite monoliths by the late Texas-based sculptor Jesus Bautista Moroles by the office entrance.

Running down the slope from Moroles's monoliths is "William's Walk." The wife had wanted a way to stroll through the sagebrush. Peters hesitated for a couple of days after receiving her assignment, then one morning plunged in, Felco pruning shears in hand, in his attempt to "choreograph" the stroller's experience.

He used the contours of the land to pace the stroll: "If you come to a portion of the walk that is narrower and steeper," he explains,

Sprouting from the turf like giant stone puffballs, these sculptures the owners acquired in Korea have settled easily into the Idaho mountainside.

"you're going to slow down and be more thoughtful. You'll watch your step." When the path approached a view Peters wanted to exclude, he turned it uphill or downhill. While climbing or descending, walkers must focus their eyes on their feet. As the path arrives at a more desirable view, Peters has flattened it again. Walking becomes easier, so that the stroller relaxes and reflexively looks up. A turn, Peters notes, can reinforce this. "A turn makes you turn your eyes, and it also makes you slow down. It makes you focus." These devices control the stroller's mood, directing the eye continually from the town below to the superb peaks that fill the horizon.

A crucial punctuation for the walk was supplied by the owners. They were fascinated with the stone-worshipping cultures that built Stonehenge and other prehistoric sites. One day they had driven down to Nevada and brought back three monoliths. The owners laugh at the memory: They purchased the stones from old

> "We did something that was inspired by the land.
> If we did it right, you go there and you think, wow...."
>
> —WILLIAM PETERS

mining claims whose prospector-owners clearly thought they were mad. But how could the prospectors resist? By selling stones to the mad Idahoans for $100 apiece, they were legally mining the claims and thus satisfying the government's requirement for continued possession.

Set up along the path, the rugged stones bring a more comfortable, human scale to the mountainside's awesome sweep. At the same time, they produce an effect that the Japanese call *shakkei*: that is, the garden stones "borrow" from the distant scenery. First they capture the eye, then they jump it from their own miniature peaks to the real ones in the distance. The effect is to bring the entire valley into the garden.

Nature provides color. Flushes of wildflowers turn the garden orange, yellow, and blue in turn. William Peters loves it best in autumn, though, when only the sunlit gold of the aspen leaves interrupts the tonalities of gray and brown. But if the garden changes with the season, it also changes with the time of day. In the morning, the monoliths have a more dramatic presence. Viewed from the house, they are backlighted, so they stand dark against the sun-bleached, gray-green sage.

The garden-makers admit to having changed the look of the mountainside. Over time, they have groomed the sagebrush by removing deadwood; by weeding out the coarsest of the wild grasses, they have gradually refined the landscape's texture. At the same time, the landscape has left its mark on them.

For the owners, coming into harmony with the site's austerity brought about a simplification of their own style. The potted plants, for instance, formerly placed around the exterior of the house, have been removed, so there is no competition with the vista.

For William Peters, the project was a form of letting go. This garden is not the traditional English cottage garden we all were taught to make. In Sun Valley, he learned to work boldly with nature. He learned to be as ruthless as nature when he should be. At the same time, he learned a sort of selflessness.

"We did something that was inspired by the land. If we did it right, you go there and you think, Wow, this is really cool. But you really don't know what we did. That was our journey."

Rugged monoliths gathered off a Nevada mining claim help to direct the walk below the house, while connecting the garden to the surrounding peaks.

STEVE MARTINO

Arizona

It was a brush with the law that introduced Steve Martino to his love of the wild. A precocious if badly behaved 12-year-old, Martino was stealing cars, "that sort of thing," and had been expelled from parochial school. He was given a choice between reform school and the boot-camp-like program of the Arizona Boys Ranch. He chose the latter and spent the next four and a half years at the ranch's remote campus in the Sonoran Desert. At the time, most Arizonans regarded the desert as wasteland, something that any change would improve. Martino came to know differently. Gradually, he became aware of the beauty and the inherent order in that landscape, and began the study that has absorbed him ever since.

Attitudes toward the desert have changed, but Phoenix, the city in which Martino has chosen to pursue his career as a landscape architect, remains missionary country. Despite Arizona's chronic problems with water shortages, turf is still the ground cover of choice through much of this desert capital, and Phoenix residents keep it emerald green by flooding a whole yard with an inch or more of water on a weekly basis. "We could be anywhere," Martino complains, gesturing toward one of these conventional landscapes. "We could be in Palm Beach."

No one could make that mistake about any of the gardens Martino has created for his host of private, public, and corporate clients. His work is grounded in the region's landscape. The city boasts numerous landscapers who make a gesture toward that— they set a saguaro cactus and a cluster of rocks in front of a house and call it desert-scaping. Martino really knows and loves the

OPPOSITE
The prickly pear, one of Steve Martino's favorite plants, embodies the prickly beauty of the desert that this landscape architect prizes.

desert flora. What's more, he understands the way it likes to grow and how that conflicts with the design patterns Anglo-Americans brought to this state.

Martino first became aware of the design potential of the desert plants while taking time off from the architecture program at Arizona State University. He was working for a landscape architect laying sod, and looked over at the vacant lot next door, where all the plants were flourishing. Snapping a branch off one of these plants, he asked his boss why they couldn't use it in their landscape. Because it was a weed, he was told, and no one could tell him more about his find until he eventually met a young nurseryman named Ron Gass, who shared his enthusiasm for the native plants. Martino went to work for Gass, and together they more or less invented the local trade in native plants, collecting seeds from the desert to establish the cultivated stocks Martino needed for the landscape designs he had started to create.

Martino never returned to school for formal training in landscape architecture or design. Instead, he says, he studied at the arroyo, the desert wash. Runoff from the occasional rains collects in these channels, sinking into gravelly beds that the deep-rooted desert plants can tap even weeks later. "The wash is where the action is in the desert," Martino says. "It is where the animals like to be, and the plants there are lush and mysterious."

Martino quickly moved from studying individual plants to noticing how they associated one with another. He came to understand that gardening rules of thumb developed in England and the Northeast did not apply here. The Sonoran flora is exceptionally rich: acre per acre, there is a much greater diversity of species than one might find in an apparently lush northeastern woodland. In part, the plants have adapted to the lower rainfall by spacing themselves more widely and by growing as individuals rather than as part of a mass. The traditional horticultural practice of planting in drifts is not appropriate here; besides creating a need for excessive irrigation, it simply looks unnatural. Nor are ground covers appropriate to the desert. There isn't enough water to support a blanket of greenery, for though the desert plants do infiltrate broadly through the soil, they do so underground, with a network of roots that are protected from the sun.

The native look as handled by Martino—lots of bare earth, lots of hardscape—is not sparse, but is instead elegantly spare. It requires exceptional sensitivity and care in the placement and balancing of the various elements. In the courtyard that he planted for

> "Where you have a wall, it lifts shadows from the ground and makes them visible."
>
> —STEVE MARTINO

a local paper, the *New Times*, he set the mesquite trees, ironwoods, sweet acacias, and palo verde trees not on elevations à la Capability Brown, but in depressions, where he excavated channels to collect and feed rainwater to them. On another site, he set a feathery-leaved palo verde tree in front of a wall: "Where you have a wall, it lifts shadows from the ground and makes them visible. They become architectural ornaments." In a similar vein, he backed one garden with a curved, lavender-colored wall, and projected onto it shadows of agaves and prickly pears.

The plants themselves are architectural. Strong and assertive, they call for similar treatment from the gardener. Dropped in among the plantings, a blue pyramid and a white concrete orb make a strong statement in one of his gardens. Martino selected a searing yellow color to paint the wall that ran up the back boundary of the yard of Jim Larkin, publisher of the *New Times*. Elsewhere this would have been too much, but here, less would be not enough. The intense desert sunlight drains the strength from colors, so the hues must be strong to hold their own. The wall also blocks out the jumble of rocks and vegetation around the yard that would confuse and weaken the view. While he was at it, Martino made the wall work in another way, cutting out a gap that functions as an outdoor fireplace and folding down a bright blue flight of stairs to give access to a dining space.

Martino's take on nature is admiring and affectionate, but not reflexively reverential. He is known as an authority on native plants and has been employed as a designer for Phoenix's famous Desert Botanic Garden. Yet he takes issue with native-plants purists who would root up non native trees even in areas where they flourish and where the shade is desperately needed. Martino is, at heart, still something of a bad boy; he bristles at the notion of following someone else's rules.

No doubt that is why he feels so much at home where he is, in an extreme landscape where the enduring rules are so obviously not man's but nature's. Martino likes to measure himself by those standards. His affection for the prickly ocotillo or Indian fig is plainly familial.

OPPOSITE
A pool, set in a ring of dark tile like a desert spring amid the rocks, turns a corner of the terrace into an oasis.

ABOVE
The architectural desert plants are ideal for display in an architectural setting.

LEFT
Only strong colors can stand up to the brilliant southwestern sun; the yellow of this wall is borrowed from the plants above, establishing a link between man's space and nature.

OVERLEAF
With an enclosing wall and native plantings, Martino has worked a delightful deception: this garden seems a comfortable corner of wilderness, though in fact it is surrounded by a housing development.

DAN PEARSON
England

Trust your first impression, Dan Pearson says. It is your clearest reading of "the sense of a place and its mood," and respecting that, according to the English horticultural prodigy, is the crux of design. Or, at least, of the design that has made Pearson famous.

Pearson remembers the first instant he saw the land that would become a garden on the South Downs of Britain's Sussex coast. He came over the crest of a hill, and there, set into the slope below, was the house. Beyond and all around was a vast sweep of nibbled grassland. The client's property itself was compact, but it was set into a huge tract that belonged to the National Trust, with land running off, uninterrupted, for miles—all the way to the English Channel. Pearson remembers an impression of the "soft curves of the land, the gentle mounds, and the wonderful turf, sadly derelict, overgrown, and full of tiny wild orchids, cowslips, primrose, and bird's-foot trefoil." The view was serene and the topography sensual, but the gentle appearance proved to be deceptive. With nothing to stop the sea winds, only small rugged trees such as hawthorns could survive without protection.

Pearson has become a celebrity through his work as a weekly columnist for the *Sunday Times* of London and for the *Telegraph*, as a best-selling author, and as the former host of a popular television series featuring his design wisdom. Like all celebrities, he projects a strong image. His designs, it is said, are "plant driven." It is a fact that Pearson's background is in the hands-on side of gardening. Having been a gardener since childhood, he has a vivid memory of the time when he was six years old and his father made

OPPOSITE

A walled garden that Dan Pearson created for a set-designer client is simple, yet appropriately dramatic. Red corn poppies sown into the gravel paths give an untamed look.

a pond for him; he recalls, too, the yellow border that he subsequently planted in the family garden. Later, he took courses at the Royal Horticultural Society Garden at Wisley, then at the Edinburgh Botanical Garden, and finally at the Royal Botanic Gardens at Kew. While completing this all-star curriculum, he also took trips into the wild to see how the plants grew on their own. Pearson plants not in beds and borders, but in habitats. His personal quest has been to reconcile the wildness that fascinates him with the man-made environments in which he plies his craft.

That's apparent in the South Downs garden's plant list. In the meadows with which he surrounded this composition, Pearson was careful to use only native species. The planting civilizes as it approaches the client's residence; perennials give way to brighter, more domesticated biennial and annual flowers. In a courtyard enclosed by two wings of the house, there is even space for promiscuous exotics.

While paying tribute to Pearson's plantsmanship, it would be a mistake to discount his mastery of landforms and composition. His treatment of the site was respectful, but since the client is a theatrical set designer, it was suitably dramatic. He reshaped the slope on which the house sat, pushing the crest away from the house, and in the process scooped out a hollow for an open-air amphitheater. He designed this in cooperation with the client, who made a plaster-of-Paris model that the two men then trimmed and adjusted with blows of an ax. An ellipse of turf became the stage, and for seating, Pearson constructed some tiered, bench-high walls made of the local flint that he wrapped around one side of the stage. Up above, Pearson heaped the earth into a "bosomy" profile, forming low hummocks that mimic the surrounding hills.

Reconfiguring the hillside also created shelter from the persistent winds. On the whole, though, Pearson is not a controlling gardener. He refrains from unnecessary interference, preferring to let the plants set seed and sow themselves where they will. In this way, they gradually select the spots that suit them best and the garden retains a fresh unpredictability. In the South Downs garden he stayed true to his native theme by using indigenous materials—locally obtained gravel, old railroad ties, and local brick. The frame is especially prominent in the spaces that Pearson created next to the house, within the perimeter of an old walled kitchen garden. There he laid out an ornamental pool, flowers, and vegetables in nearly uniform rectangular beds, and a small orchard in a simple grid pattern. So regular is the overall pattern that it might

have seemed oppressive if not for the free-form ribbon of corn poppies that weaves back and forth through the gravel paths.

Plants and their needs are important here, but always in the
context of human space. The meadows, for instance, are a salute to
the downs, but broad paths mowed into them make a place for
walks, too, or for sitting. A turf seat, a bench surfaced with grass,
has been set into the garden's northern corner, and around the
bend there is a tiny echo of the amphitheater, an intimate sunken
space centered on a fire pit.

It is a give-and-take, this garden—a continual exchange
between man and plant, domesticated and wild. A less expert gardener might have worried about weeds overwhelming his meadows,
but Pearson knew that the site's chalky soil called for yarrow and
wild yellow mignonette, teasel and mallow. He sowed these and a
couple of dozen other adapted species of grasses and flowers. But
Pearson also counts on nature's contributions; he looks forward to
the gradual infiltration of wild marjoram and thyme from the hills.
Embracing the wild is Dan Pearson's way of taming a place.

ABOVE

A path mown through the meadow
takes the stroller to a secluded, semi-
circular turf seat focused on a fire pit.

RIGHT

A naturalistic style can be formal, as
this corner of the walled garden
shows. The massed boxwoods will be
sheared into large squares to mimic
the geometry of the pool. Poppies and
strawberries sprouting unbidden at
the pool's foot furnish the essential
element of spontaneity.

OVERLEAF

A miniature amphitheater cut into a
grassy slope is a striking bit of land art,
and a performance space for the client.

PART FOUR **THE
PLANTSMEN**

FEATURED DESIGNERS
IN THIS SECTION:

JOHN GWYNNE AND MIKEL FOLCARELLI
New England

JAY GRIFFITH
California

WOLFGANG OEHME AND JAMES VAN SWEDEN
Massachusetts

PIET OUDOLF
The Netherlands

CHRISTOPHER LLOYD
England

PART FOUR INTRODUCTION

There are those who believe that the tail should always wag the dog. For most of us, the idea of a garden arises from a simple inspiration, a simple desire. To satisfy this desire, a garden is planned and finally, to suit the plan, catalogs are spread out on the table and appropriate plants are chosen. For the plantsmen, though, this process is reversed. Plantsmen build their gardens from the ground up, quite literally. For them, gardens start with a cutting or a division or, more often, with seeds.

Rarity is an ultimate virtue in the plantsmen's eyes. What they seek is, ideally, something no one else has. Some plantsmen become fixated on assembling every permutation within a particular set—all the ferns native to a particular region, perhaps, or all the species of tulips. More common, however, are the connoisseurs who seek the very best of each breed. Plantsmanship comes down to the pursuit of the special and the rare, of things that cannot be found in a pot at the local garden center. If these treasures are found in a friend's garden (the place that the rest of us might go to beg or steal a start), plantsmen no longer want them; they are too easily available. To get what they want, plantsmen must travel and patronize eccentric boutique nurseries (preferably by mail) or the seed exchanges of specialized plant societies. True plantsmen grow their own.

PREVIOUS PAGES
A horticultural landmark dating from 1910, the gardens at Great Dixter continue to change thanks to the insatiable plantsmanship of Christopher Lloyd.

OPPOSITE
The plantsman's knowledge of ecology and plant adaptation can result in extraordinarily rich combinations, as is shown in this detail of a Dutch garden by Piet Oudolf.

Their gardens are, in general, appalling. They are, after all, arranged to serve the needs of the plants, and commonly are full of strange and awkward expedients: pop-up sprinklers and misting nozzles to increase humidity around certain specimens, or, to enhance drainage and reduce humidity, raised beds fashioned from cinder blocks, old tires, or worse. In extreme cases, the plants may never touch the earth—one of the world's greatest connoisseurs of heirloom roses kept his collection in five-gallon plastic buckets lined up on a gravel parking lot. The effect, incidentally, was surprisingly powerful: the squalor of their surroundings cast into greater relief the exquisite elegance of the blossoms.

There are the exceptions, though. Occasionally, there are plantsmen who connect with the collection, connoisseurs who see beyond collectibility to understand the plants at a deeper level. Their gardens are among the most miraculous of landscapes, improbable privatized Edens where anything seems possible. In them, you discover what nature might have done if it had had the restraint.

Six hundred years before the beginning of the modern era, Nebuchadnezzar II of Babylon was stacking masonry walls one atop the other so that in the artificial heights he could grow the mountain flora his Iranian wife was missing. Forerunner of the contemporary rock gardener, the king epitomized one strain of plantsmanship, the do-it-yourself ecologist. He was creating not just a garden but a habitat, or rather the dream of a habitat, his own world as the world ought to be.

A simple acquisitive itch is also key to the activities of most plantsmen. Daniel Hinkley, founder of Heronswood Nursery and the most famous of modern plant collectors, was asked in an interview a couple of years ago about the number of taxa (botanically distinct types of plants) in his collection. He admitted to a list of 10,000 species, varieties, and clones, but hastened to add that the total

would soon increase, with the germination of the 700 seed samples he had just brought back from an eleven-week trip through Turkey and mainland China.

Hinkley had cogent reasons why every one of these plants could be important. Some belonged to species never before seen in gardens, and could add a new dimension to our planting. Others were genetically distinct representatives of species already in cultivation, and might be able to contribute new and valuable traits (different flower colors, for example; greater resistance to cold or disease) to the strains already on the market. When asked if his current collection was not sufficient to keep him busy for the foreseeable future, Hinkley said no. He was preparing for his trip to the Salween River on the border of China and Burma, an area, Hinkley said, so isolated that it has never been disturbed by human activity.

Yet human activity is what gardening is all about, and so too is plantsmanship. Where other gardeners may be content to argue in

Knowing just the right plant for each spot, and the spot for each plant, is the plantsman's trademark. This marriage of alliums and delphiniums in a corner of Great Dixter could hardly be bettered.

Curbing the appetite for plants to make space for beauty and comfort is the plantsman's greatest challenge, one met admirably in the garden Jay Griffith created in collaboration with Brad Pitt.

English, or some other vernacular, the plantsmen hew to their dead language. "I particularly recall a *splendidum*," Mikel Folcarelli has written of the orchid that was the pretext for his first meeting with partner and plantsman John Gwynne. "He remembers it as a *magnificum*."

I say potato, you say *Solanum tuberosum*. Such arguments are endless, and plantsmen enjoy nothing more than visiting a competitor's garden and explaining why their identifications are mistaken. Disagreement appears to be an essential part of the creative process for the plantsman. "Collaborative confrontations" is the more tactful term that landscape designer Jay Griffith uses for this aspect of his long professional association with actor Brad Pitt.

The ability to dream like a child, never to fully grasp that imagining something does not necessarily make it so, can be a powerful constructive force. When this is coupled with sufficient practical experience and energy, the result can be an achievement that the mature, rational individual would know better than to attempt. Would any adult in his right mind have looked at the uptight lawns and foundation plantings of 1970s America and decided, as James

ABOVE

The single-minded vision of the plantsman can be a powerful force. The vision of James van Sweden and Wolfgang Oehme has replaced the American fashion for neatly trimmed lawns into one for flowing sweeps of uncut grasses and flowers.

van Sweden and Wolfgang Oehme did thirty years ago, that they must be replaced with flowing sweeps of uncut grasses and flowers? And then make it happen?

Sharing a garden is not an easy thing. It commonly ends in a divorce, without shared custody. This makes it notable that so many of the great plantsmen's gardens (and all except one of those featured here) are joint efforts.

Aside from making arguments and discussions available around the clock, partnering can solve the inherent conflict of the plantsmen's gardens. No one knows how to garden better than the plantsmen, if only they will let themselves do it. Having grown everything, or at least as big a share of everything that they can acquire, they know better than anyone the exact spot for each species, and the species for each spot. They know the plant that is equal to each environmental challenge, to each aesthetic need. Plantsmen would plant the right plant every time, if only they could limit themselves to planting just one. That is the function of the partner: to be the interfering and affectionate critic; to make sure that no opportunities are wasted and that beauty is served.

JOHN GWYNNE AND MIKEL FOLCARELLI

New England

For John Gwynne, the garden is a natural counterpart to his working life. During the week it's fauna; on weekends, flora. Gwynne, a landscape architect, is head of exhibitions at the Wildlife Conservation Society's Bronx Zoo—it's his job to create effective and authentic displays of one of the world's great collections of animal life. Plants are accessories there, but they take center stage as soon as he can slip away to his house on the New England coast. For twenty years, Gwynne has been installing in an acre of woodland a series of plant collections that, taken together, present a vision of the world as rich and astonishingly exotic as anything to be found in a zoo.

He has had help. He has shared most of the garden's life with Mikel Folcarelli, vice president of international creative services for Ralph Lauren. Folcarelli is, in the garden, the perfect complement to Gwynne, who serves as the plant omnivore, a collector who wants the best of everything, from the paperbark maple (*Acer griseum*) of China, with its peeling cinnamon skin, to tree yuccas, wild Peruvian lilies, Japanese black-stemmed bamboos, and giant parasol-leaved South American gunneras. Folcarelli has contributed not only an insistence on style, but also a focus on know-how. The self-described "grandson of a talented and sensitive Italian gardener," he worried about improving the heavy clay soil, kept an eye on watering, and made sure that a compromise was struck between where a plant would look best and where it would actually survive.

There is an undercurrent of quirky humor running through this garden. Gwynne is piqued by oddities—a spot was found for the strange sugar maple ('Monumentale') "that doesn't seem interested in growing side branches." Sometimes the shipments of what Gwynne describes as "coffin-sized cardboard boxes," dispatched from little-known nurseries, drove Folcarelli to mock despair. Gwynne was testing limits, growing palmettos and camellias in the open air in USDA zone six.

Given his history, though, no one could be more conscious of the distinction between a menagerie and a collection than Gwynne; what he was assembling is most definitely the latter. It is, in fact, not one but a complex of collections. In what they call the "tropical bog," for example, they grow 100 species of Asian arisaemas, larger, more flamboyant versions of the native jack-in-the-pulpit. Even more impressive, the heart of the garden is the "rhododendron punch bowl." Around a keyhole-shaped lawn, Gwynne has gathered a variety of uncommon rhododendrons, sorts almost unknown in the heyday of the great estates with their plant connoisseurs back in the 1920s and 1930s. Tree-sized Himalayan specimens stand in an outer ring, with smaller types in front to create an amphitheater of evergreen foliage and, from mid-spring to early summer, glorious bloom. Two child-sized red chairs set in the center play tricks with the perspective, suggesting that the ring is larger than it actually is.

In addition to botanically themed collections, there are those that center on a color or texture. There is a moss garden, for example, and a silver meadow in which grayish grasses and herbs intermingle with white delphinium and foxglove and wild geranium to make a scene that the midday sun dissolves into a shimmery opalescent glare. There are the red borders, a yellow circle, and an orange grove—actually a woodland opening of true lilies mixed with orange-flowered Peruvian lilies (*Alstroemeria*).

Integrating so many disparate elements presented two challenges. The first was horticultural—that of creating microclimates, niches of special conditions, so that plants of such varying origins could thrive side by side. The two men achieved this in large part with windbreaks. They planted a network of hedges, lining them with walls of six-foot-high snow fence that provided shelter while the walls of shrubbery were establishing themselves. By blocking out the winter air that blows in from the north and west, the windbreaks keep the garden at the milder norm of this seaside area. "On a raw, April day," Gwynne notes, "the garden will be as much as ten to twenty degrees warmer than the adjacent fields."

The careful arrangement of different rhododendrons by size has turned this circular area into a gloriously blooming "punch bowl" every May.

Barriers also furnished shelter from winter sun, something that, counterintuitively, is likely to prove fatal to marginally hardy evergreens. By warming and temporarily thawing buds and foliage, the sun creates another opportunity for frost damage when it sets in late afternoon and temperatures plunge. Gwynne and Folcarelli have found, for example, that camellias (classically considered to be hardy only in Washington, D.C.) will die if planted on the south side of a hedge, but thrive a few feet away on the north side.

The second major challenge of this garden was one of design, of making the wildly disparate elements cohere. The hedges provided a solution for this, too, by dividing the garden into discrete spaces or rooms. Each collection within the collection could then be given a room of its own. "Each space," Gwynne explains, "has its own plants, shape, and distinct feeling, in large part because it is separated from the others by the high walls."

To order the experiences, Gwynne and Folcarelli arranged the rooms along what amounted to halls, running a formal, axial format of paths and cross paths through the wooded site. In this way, they could control the order in which the rooms were visited, and so play one off against the other. From the glossy-leaved formality of the rhododendron punch-bowl, for example, you cross directly to the tactile sensuality of the moss garden, then make a right and find yourself in the incandescent splendor of the orange grove. The sense of anticipation this arouses propels the visitor forward, curious always to see what lies through the next gap. The extreme diversity of the planting has been transformed into an asset by Gwynne and Folcarelli.

The garden, of course, will never be finished. Gwynne and Folcarelli continue to refine the plant combinations in their rooms, most recently experimenting with the introduction of touches of deliberately clashing colors. This, they say, follows a theory proposed by the great Edwardian English designer Gertrude Jekyll, who insisted that clashing colors injected extra energy into a scene. So, among the chartreuse nicotianas, green spider daylilies, and golden-leaved elderberries and tansies of the yellow garden, they have begun to set flowers of grape purple. Even on a dark day, they say, this room seems to glow.

But of course the quest for the ultimate rarity hasn't ended. Gwynne wonders why the contrasts have to come from juxtaposing different plants. Isn't there, somewhere, a plant that clashes perfectly with itself? A yellow-foliaged *Clematis viticella*, maybe, with small dark plum bells? "Always something more to dream about," says Folcarelli.

OPPOSITE
Folcarelli and Gwynne found a perfect match in the combination of a Chinese paperbark maple (Acer griseum), with its peeling cinnamon bark, and an orange-blossomed, wild form of the Peruvian lily (Alstroemeria aurantiaca).

ABOVE
An Asian relative of jack-in-the-pulpit lends an exotic note to the woodland floor.

RIGHT
The "orange grove," a haven for orange-colored flowers and barks, faces open fields beyond. In spring, mobs of flesh-colored daffodils give it another character.

ABOVE
Connoisseurs of foliage, Folcarelli and Gwynne created a piquant juxtaposition with golden-leaved bleeding heart (Dicentra spectabilis 'Gold Heart') and variegated butterbur (Petasites japonicus 'Variegatus').

OPPOSITE
A dramatic contrast in forms was combined with a harmony of colors when ivory-flowered Rhododendron 'Bellringer' was planted alongside yellow-groove bamboo.

OVERLEAF
Surrounding hedges protect the garden spaces from winter winds by creating milder microclimates. They also provide a reassuring sense of enclosure.

JAY GRIFFITH

California

Off the record, the West Coast landscape architect complained that actors (a large part of his business) didn't really want him to make them a garden. What they wanted was just another studio set. But he had never worked with Brad Pitt. When it comes to garden design, you do actually work with Pitt, as Jay Griffith discovered. Much in demand, Griffith is a Santa Monica–based landscape designer who founded with Pitt what amounts to their own horticultural Fight Club.

They first met when Pitt, in the course of a house-hunting expedition, was taken to Griffith's Santa Monica home and was "blown away by the garden." Pitt waited for the owner to return, then launched into a dialogue with the designer. "Jay was rude, cantankerous; I was really taken with him." When Pitt finally did locate the house he was looking for, he renewed contact with Griffith.

The arguments that followed were passionate. Although Pitt may have been new to gardening, he took on the role of designer with characteristic commitment. Griffith was impressed by his new client's intelligence and discerning eye. Over time they worked out a routine, which, according to Pitt, works this way:

Step 1: Pitt tells Griffith about an idea.
Step 2: Griffith tells Pitt why it can't be done.
Step 3: They argue, but resolve their differences when
    Griffith works out a counterproposal that far exceeds what
    Pitt had originally hoped for.
Step 4: They return to Step 1 and the cycle begins again.

OPPOSITE
Griffith's fine taste for textures plays the swordlike leaves of furcraea against the finely cut Artemisia arboresecens *and the threadlike Mexican weeping bamboo, a complementary match that emboldens each element.*

"Jay was rude, cantankerous; I was really taken with him."

—BRAD PITT

What Pitt had originally hoped for was a Japanese garden. This made sense in light of the house that he had selected, a 1911 vintage Arts and Crafts house on a small property in the Hollywood Hills. The ethnicity of the garden was suggested to Pitt by the house; the Craftsman style of building borrowed heavily from Japanese architecture.

Too obvious, responded Griffith.

Instead, he suggested an Asian-inspired garden assembled from plants suited to Los Angeles's very un-Japanese climate: native Californian plants as well as species from the dry lands of the Mediterranean basin and Australia.

Griffith and Pitt generated an Asian spirit through their calm, considered use of these plants; they avoided the bright floral effects of Western gardens. There is plenty of drama here—Pitt cannot seem to avoid that either in his films or in his personal life—but there are few blossoms. Instead, there is delight in countless shades of green worked into a rich and cooling collage. This is a garden very much of its region. People passing through Los Angeles, stopping off for a few days, a week, or a few years to do business, may not grasp how precious green is in naturally semidesert southern California. Without the water pumped over mountains from the distant Colorado River, Los Angeles's hills and valleys would be brown most of the year. Millions of sprinkler heads make sure that this is no longer so, but a gardener of vision understands that water must not be taken for granted.

Green on green. Griffith and Pitt have brought in the lush, emerald green of turf for the open spaces of lawn; polished jade for the trunks and canopy of the palms; blue-green of *Artemisia* 'Powis Castle' that edges the water of the pool. Even the necessary contrasts, the accents of red or yellow that were needed to enliven the composition, come from foliage rather than blossoms: spike-leaved New Zealand flaxes rising like a Dr. Seuss balustrade around the tiled patio next to the house, a ribbon of crotons spilling in a lurid cascade alongside the sheeting water of a fountain. A reference, in season, to the native color scheme may be found in the feathered sweeps of head-high ornamental grasses that clothe one hillside. Green during the moisture of spring, these age to real southern California gold as the sun and heat dry out the landscape in summer.

OPPOSITE

Crotons and New Zealand flax (Phormium tenax *'Guardsman') supplied the tropical setting Brad Pitt wanted for this cascade-cum-pool; the blue foliage of* Artemisia *'Powis Castle' enhances and plays off the color of the water.*

Brad Pitt's request for a Japanese garden inspired this original land-scape, one that is definitely Asian in feel but also uniquely personal.

Ribbons of green were also used to stitch together the ever-expanding landscape; as Pitt's interest in garden-making grew, he began purchasing adjacent properties, demolishing the houses or incorporating them in what was fast becoming an estate. To reach the guesthouse, which was captured in this manner, the lucky visitor explores a parsley-hued tunnel of tree ferns and papyrus.

There are touches of sly humor. The classic Japanese technique of "borrowing scenery," of framing a view so explicitly that the distant objects are made part of the garden, has been applied here to a vista of the famous Hollywood sign. Overall, the feeling is one of a calm masculinity at one with the owner. The muscular trunk of a eucalyptus or huge yucca, the swordlike yellow-streaked leaves of a giant furcraea, pose in virile fashion that anyone other than Pitt might envy.

A marble cascade, made-to-order travertine pagodas—there is an unashamedly theatrical aspect to this garden. Yet it saves itself from mere posturing by its emphasis on great naturalistic sweeps of plants—the tall grasses, groves of bamboo, knee-deep carpets of ferns. This is far more than another set. This is, as Pitt respectfully describes it, "a gallery of God's best work."

ABOVE
Sword ferns and spires of Cordyline australis *'Red Star' enhance the exotic detailing of Brad Pitt's Arts and Crafts house.*

OPPOSITE
Artemisia and the overhanging pennisetums lend an air of mystery and romance to a path that seems purposely headed toward Hollywood.

Senecio mandraliscae *borders a pool in blue. When Pitt could not find an authentic pagoda to suit this area of the garden, Griffith had a modern interpretation crafted in the same travertine used to restore the house.*

WOLFGANG OEHME AND
JAMES VAN SWEDEN

Massachusetts

Bold, *Romantic Gardens* is the title James van Sweden gave to
a book he wrote about the landscapes he and Wolfgang
Oehme have created together. A boldness of pattern and
color, presumably, is what he meant, but there is courage, too, in
their design. Only a courageous designer could have faced up to the
challenges of this eighty-five-acre property on the Nantucket shore.

It's a dream site, with some of the most spectacular views on the
East Coast of North America, and a handsomely crafted, gray-shin-
gled house designed by architects Edward and Mary Knowles. The
challenges to any sort of horticultural gesture, though, were formida-
ble. The soil was almost pure sand, lacking in nutrients and quick to
dry. Enhancing this tendency to drought was the lack of shelter—
any moisture a plant might try to hoard would be blown away by
the ocean winds, or evaporated by the brilliant sunlight. Every storm
swept the site with plant-toxic salt spray, and whatever greenery did
persist was soon nibbled down by the island's year-round residents—
the local rabbits and deer. The owners of the house had tried, without success, to impose some sort of landscaping for four years when
they finally called in Oehme and van Sweden.

Founding partners of Oehme, van Sweden and Associates, these
two are plantsmen in the most fundamental sense. Their design
style is rooted in the needs and inspiration of the plants. Their
goal, of course, is to create a comfortable and attractive landscape,
something suited to the clients' needs; but because the plants are
the agents by which this is effected, Oehme and van Sweden know
that they must please them as well.

OPPOSITE

*Openness and sweep are the chief
beauties of this eighty-five-acre seaside site and its greatest challenge
to designers Oehme and van Sweden.
The solution they found lay in a
planting inspired by the dune-
dwelling grasses and wildflowers.*

Raising a low berm around the house, Oehme and van Sweden deflected the fierce coastal winds, creating protection for man and plants, without obscuring the views.

> "When dealing with winds and salt spray and the views, you want that sheared feeling you get along the ocean."
>
> —JAMES VAN SWEDEN

That, claims van Sweden, is what Wolfgang Oehme would do in any case. The German-born Oehme apprenticed as a nurseryman before studying landscape architecture at the University of Berlin. A personal friend and disciple of the great German plantsman Karl Foerster, Oehme brought a pocketful of ideas and seeds with him when he immigrated to the United States in the late 1950s. His nagging and the market he created for innovative plants played a huge role in expanding the offerings of nurseries around his new home in Baltimore; in particular he helped to spark an explosion of interest in ornamental grasses. For van Sweden (who formally joined forces with Oehme in 1975), the plants are objects of beauty; for Oehme, they are more in the nature of personal friends, and despite the firm's enormous success, he still spends most of his days with a trowel, on his knees, planting.

Though van Sweden is an expert plantsman himself, his essential contribution to the partnership has been his artist's sensibility. His first study of landscape design was over an easel, as a teenager painting and drawing the meadows and dunes along the shore of Lake Michigan. This, together with three and a half years' study of landscape architecture in the Netherlands (van Sweden is of Dutch descent), produced a strong affinity for horizontal landscapes. He felt immediately at home on the Nantucket site.

Their first order of business was to create the pocket of shelter that both plant and human residents craved. The challenge, as van Sweden saw it, was to accomplish this without blocking the views. Gently massaging the land, he raised a low berm around the house, creating just enough topography to divert onshore winds while obscuring no vistas other than an unwelcome one of the garage and driveway. In the gentler microclimate he had made, van Sweden and Oehme began to create their garden.

"When dealing with winds and salt spray and the views, you want to keep that sheared feeling you get along the ocean," van Sweden says. This he did through a careful selection of plant material. The dune was stabilized with native beach grasses and wildflowers. The rest of the planting followed from this initial statement, though the emphasis on native species was relaxed in the interest of giving the garden a richer, more cultivated look. Feather reed grass (*Calamagrostis acutiflora* 'Stricta'), Japanese Hakone grass (*Hakonechloa macra*), tufted hairgrass (*Deschamp-*

OPPOSITE
White plumes of Persicaria polymorpha *lend a foreground to this view from the entryway; the grass-covered enclosing mound serves as background, hiding the guest cottages beyond.*

sia caespitosa), Moroccan fescue (*Festuca mairei*), and an Asian fountain grass (*Pennisetum alopecuroides* 'Hameln') were mixed with native American switchgrass (*Panicum virgatum*) in a cosmopolitan prairie that, when stirred by the breeze, mimicked the waves rolling into the beach beyond.

Generous swaths of perennials—*Achillea* 'Coronation Gold,' *Iris siberica* 'Caesar's Brother,' *Persicaria polymorpha*, and *Allium giganteum*—filled the area around the house, intermingling at the edges, one species shading imperceptibly into another in a dynamic tapestry that laps right up against the house. A burst of poppies, a drift of salvia, might emphasize the route of a path, but there are no beds and borders in this scheme.

Developing the design in partnership with the plants pays many dividends. Selecting bitter-tasting species such as the achillea has made the garden unappealing to the deer and rabbits. Using drought-tolerant, vigorous plants and letting them establish themselves in something like their natural complex tapestries means that, once the garden has taken root, there is little need for weeding. There is an ebb and flow to the plantings as various species gradually seek out the areas best suited to them, but the fabric of the garden remains intact, leaving no room for weeds. Nor is there any need for deadheading and clipping, which would be a disservice to this garden. The seed heads of the perennials and the tasseled flowers of the grasses, drying on their stems, are beautiful in the fall and winter, and provide food for a host of birds.

This is a garden designed for the enjoyment of its human inhabitants: there's room for a croquet lawn, and the bench by the front door is canopied with sweet-scented *Clematis paniculata*. The setting has been respected; nature has been enhanced, not violated.

ABOVE

The plants that envelop the guest cottages were so carefully chosen and look so at home that it is hard to imagine that the planting was done by man.

OPPOSITE

No barrier could be allowed to interrupt such magnificent visual sweeps. The island's voracious deer were discouraged by planting species they find unpalatable.

White-blossomed Clematis paniculata *threads its way in through the trellis that encloses the entryway, weaving a canopy over a cedar bench by Michigan artist Clifton Monteith.*

A gayer, more intimate feel was achieved along the path around the house by wreathing the stone flags with brilliant red Oriental poppies and purple-flowered salvia.

PIET OUDOLF
The Netherlands

There is an irony to it, Piet Oudolf admits. The Netherlands, his homeland, is a country almost entirely man-made out of land rescued from the sea. Yet this Dutch nurseryman and garden designer is by common assent the most influential figure today in reintroducing the wild into our gardens. "I think maybe," Oudolf suggests, "that we [the Dutch] long more for nature, or for the unman-made land." Oudolf is internationally famous. He was the designer selected to create the "Gardens of Remembrance" in New York's Battery Park, a living memorial to the victims of the September 11, 2001 attacks, and a part of his 22-acre horticultural plan for the area. It's in England, though, that Oudolf works most often. Although an admirer of the classic English garden, Oudolf believes that the use of perennial flowers has to be "translated," in his words, to suit a new age. The English, he says, are hiring him because, for all their skill at Gertrude Jekyll-esque herbaceous borders, "they find themselves a little bit stuck."

To understand Piet Oudolf you have to see him in his native habitat. You have to put him in context, as in the garden he created for Piet and Karin Boon, principals of the design firm Piet Boon.

The site is rural, an irregular collage of field and hedgerows that contrasts pleasantly with the neatly ruled white planes of the house. It's easy to understand why the Boons selected Oudolf to design their garden, for a similar, though more dramatic, contrast is explicit in his work. The first thing to strike your eye as you enter the Boon garden is the lush romanticism of the perennial plantings and the way they have been disciplined within a simple

OPPOSITE
Surrounded by some of the most intensively cultivated countryside in the world, Piet and Karin Boon's garden nevertheless retains a surprising flavor of wildness thanks to the lush though disciplined plantings of wildflowers and grasses inserted by Piet Oudolf.

OVERLEAF
Oudolf borrowed the long, horizontal lines of the Dutch landscape and its neatly squared agricultural geometry for the garden.

"I think maybe, that we [the Dutch] long more for nature, or for the un-made land."

—PIET OUDOLF

framework of clipped hedges and rectilinear stone-paved paths and terrace. This juxtaposition is typical of Oudolf. He plans his gardens to evoke nature, but they are not wilderness; on the contrary, the energy of his landscapes derives in large part from the inherent tension between a cerebral structure and the frankly emotional plantings. It is important to note, though, that even at his most formal Oudolf is unconventional: he may organize a planting around an axial path, but in doing so he takes care to set some important element just off the expected symmetry.

Oudolf clearly knows his trees and shrubs—he is the consummate plantsman who seems always to understand which species to set where, and his choices can be brilliantly untraditional. The clipped silver roundels in front of the house have been sculpted from pear trees: *Pyrus salicifolia*, the so-called willowleaf pear, whose use as a hedging plant seems to be Oudolf's invention. But these woody plants, though essential to the garden's success, play only a supporting role. They frame the canvas of herbaceous perennials, the flowers that die back to the ground every fall and return from the roots in the spring.

Oudolf's love of the wild look has led him to avoid many of the popular garden standbys. These tend to have what Oudolf characterizes as an "overcultivated" appearance, elaborate and massive blossoms that would not harmonize with his naturalistic planting. Indeed, it was his frustration with such materials that caused Oudolf, at thirty-eight, already more than a decade into his career as a gardener, to move to the rural eastern Netherlands in 1982 and with the help of his wife, Anja, found his own nursery. There he began propagating specimens of plants that fit his vision. Often, these were species that gardeners had, for the most part, ignored, such as masterworts (*Astrantia major*) and burnets (*Sanguisorba minor*). Oudolf insisted on plants that had preserved their wild ancestors' ability to thrive without coddling.

Oudolf believes the form and the structure of a plant to be far more fundamental to its contribution than its flower color. After all, as he points out in *Designing with Plants*, co-written with Noel Kingsbury, "flower color is with us for a relatively short season."

OPPOSITE
Oudolf dislikes an overcultivated look in plants, but understands the need for domestication in living spaces. The juxtaposition of the frankly man-made with a seemingly untamed planting is what gives his gardens their understated drama.

He goes on to categorize perennial flowers not by color but rather by form: "spires," "buttons and globes," "plumes," "umbels," and so forth.

The emphasis on form, and on perennials that collaborate rather than compete, gives a remarkably architectural effect to the sort of mixed planting that can easily become an inchoate tangle. The swimming pool behind the Boons' house, for example, is given the impact of a formal reflecting pool by being flanked with a stepped progression of borders, first broad ribbons of ethereal hair grass (*Deschampsia caespitosa*) and then rising up behind them loftier moor grass (*Molinia caerulea*) and joe-pye weed (*Eupatorium purpureum* 'Atropurpureum').

This effect is carefully calculated, and Piet Oudolf is a master of detail. He is a perfectionist who distributes seed of his wild-type plants to farmers near his nursery so that, from their field-sized plantings, he can select superior, though not too domesticated, specimens to propagate for use in clients' gardens (and for sale in his nursery; some of his selections, such as *Salvia verticillata* 'Purple Rain,' have become international best sellers). Oudolf's larger quest, though, is not so cut and dried. In his gardens, he says, what he seeks is to evoke an emotion. What emotion is that? Of the "things you have lost in the city ... a feeling people long for." Trying to explain his gardens, he suggests, would be like trying to explain a poem or a book.

"A lot of people appreciate what I'm doing," Oudolf adds, most matter-of-factly. "And I don't mind if they give their own explanation to it. Whatever they think it does to them is good for me. As long as it is positive."

OPPOSITE
Structure and form rather than flower color are the characteristics by which Oudolf chooses his plants. "Flower color is with us for a relatively short season," he points out.

ABOVE

This roundel clipped from a silvery willowleaf pear seems to be an Oudolf invention. Passionately curious about plants, the Dutch designer continually looks for new material, and new uses for the familiar ones.

LEFT

Before finding his calling as a maker of gardens, Oudolf trained as an architect, a background evident in the clean-cut, abstract lines he favors.

OVERLEAF

A place to relax and for children to play, the garden Oudolf created for the Boons is also a celebration of the quiet beauty of the Dutch landscape.

CHRISTOPHER LLOYD

England

You could call Great Dixter the oldest new garden in England, though it might be more accurate to say the newest old garden. Either way, Christopher Lloyd, who has lived and gardened on these five acres nearly all of his eighty-two years, will not let it become a monument to the past. The bones of his current landscape, created for Lloyd's parents when they purchased the estate in 1910, are the work of one of Britain's most famous architects, Edwin Lutyens. Great Dixter seems an obvious candidate for the green-museum treatment that the National Trust has imposed on so many other British horticultural masterpieces. Lloyd, though, has felt free to change and develop it, so that under his care Great Dixter has become one of the most personal of great gardens. Yet he wants it to transcend even that. "I hope it will go on changing when I'm dead," he asserts. "I don't want it ever to be fossilized. And I don't want people ever to be saying, Oh, we must do this because Christopher Lloyd did it."

The secret of Great Dixter, and of Christopher Lloyd's perennial youth, seems to be twofold. Having opened the garden to the public, Lloyd entertains some 55,000 visitors a year. The height of the season he finds overwhelming, he admits, and he hides out during the day. When the crowd thins, he likes to meet the visitors and ask them about their likes and dislikes. Lloyd never loses interest—his passion for plants is as strong today as it was seven decades ago, when he traveled the adjacent countryside with his mother, collecting wild orchids to stock the meadow in front of Great Dixter's Elizabethan manor house.

OPPOSITE

Only a gardener of exceptional imagination would try to create a tropical garden as Christopher Lloyd has done in a protected place at Great Dixter. Only the most accomplished plantsman could make such a tour de force work.

OVERLEAF

Christopher Lloyd's characteristic planting—lush, sensual, and always open to fortunate accidents—is clearly visible in this view of Great Dixter's mixed borders.

His is a plantsmanship of a personal sort. Lloyd has none of the trophy-hunting, acquisitive mentality that so often marks the plantsman. Rather, he seems to be motivated by curiosity; he wants to know the qualities of each new plant he encounters. He wants to measure its potential. Lloyd develops strong likes and dislikes. He feels that roses have been elevated far above their rightful place. "I don't know why people sort of worship at them. And say: 'Oh, I don't know what I'm going to have in my garden, but of course I must have roses.' I don't see that at all. They're very blobby shrubs. If you put a lot together, they get a lot of disease. They have an ugly habit of growth, most of them."

In this judgment, at least, Lloyd found agreement ten years ago when he took on as head gardener Fergus Garrett, the student of a horticultural professor Lloyd himself had taught when he was a lecturer at Wye College. Garrett was just back in England from a stint of working in Cap d'Antibes, and he shared Lloyd's curiosity about the potential for creating a subtropical garden in southeast England. Lloyd had just the spot: the rose garden Lutyens had designed for Lloyd's mother in 1910.

"It is the hottest part of the garden," Lloyd explains. "The roses hated it; they wilted in the sun." Lloyd had been plotting the rose garden's demise for years, and within a week of Garrett's arrival in February of 1993, Lloyd recalls, "there was a great tearing of roots Fergus entered into it with tremendous zest. Out they came. It was music to my ears, I have to say."

In part, Lloyd's desire for an "exotic garden" of tropical plants derived from his determination that Great Dixter should offer a spectacle from April—early spring—until the end of October. The tropicals and subtropicals, which relish heat, would furnish bloom in late summer, when most of the traditional perennial flowers have passed their peak, and continue on until frost.

Such a garden also offers opportunities to experiment with colors that would only look garish in the setting of a more traditional English garden. The bold tropical foliages (or tropical-seeming—Lloyd makes good use here of temperate-zone plants with outsized leaves) of the Japanese banana (*Musa basjoo*), the Chinese rice-paper plant (*Tetrapanax papyriferus*), cider gum (*Eucalyptus gunnii*), smooth sumac (*Rhus glabra* 'Laciniata'), and even tree of heaven (*Ailanthus altissima*) provide the assertive backdrop against which Lloyd can display the lurid hues of canna and dahlia blossoms and the collection of begonias that he and Fergus have amassed. It comes off as daring rather than tasteless.

Lloyd's sophisticated and daring use of color and form are evident in the glorious tapestry overlaid on the sunken garden that Edwin Lutyens created for Lloyd's parents.

Both Lloyd and Garrett are superb plantsmen, masters of the calculated effect. Yet when this lilac-flowered verbena popped up in the tropical garden, they seized on nature's offering.

The subtle yet bold handling of color and texture is typical of Lloyd and Garrett's work. But the exotic garden typifies several other points of the Great Dixter style. Like all of that landscape, this area is a palimpsest; each generation has inscribed its own story over that of its predecessors. For all his dislike of the genus, Lloyd has not removed all of the roses to which his mother and Lutyens devoted this area. Eight bushes have remained, though one suspects that when they die they will not be replaced. In similar fashion, the architectural structure for the exotic garden recalls the area's earlier use. You enter the exotic garden by passing through the "hovel," the old cattle shed, and the water feature at the exotic garden's center is the old cattle watering tank.

The other characteristic of Great Dixter is brilliant opportunism. Preoccupied as they are with the true identities of their prizes, plantsmen tend to be dictatorial gardeners. Lloyd, however, treats the plants in a far more collegial manner, welcoming "volunteers," the self-sowed seedlings that in most gardens are treated as weeds. When a lilac-flowered *Verbena bonariensis* popped up in the exotic garden, Lloyd and Garrett recognized its potential and allowed it to infuse the whole area with a haze of purple.

"I want the garden to look as though it's enjoying itself," Lloyd explains, "and one of the important things is to let plants seed themselves. Of course, we need to take out ninety-nine percent of the seedlings, but one percent will be just where we like it. So the plants, they often supply you with ideas."

This give-and-take between gardener and gardened is carried on throughout the landscape. Long ago, the dustlike seeds of the native spotted orchid blew into the Sunken Garden, establishing a colony there. When a seedling of the South African wandflower (*Dierama pulcherrimum*) popped up at the base of a topiaried yew peacock, that too was recognized as a good thing. And self-sowing is the norm in the meadow that substitutes for lawn in front of the house. (Suggest to Lloyd that he was a pioneer in the current anti-lawn movement and he laughs—his mother created the meadow under the influence of the famous Victorian "wild gardener," William Robinson.)

As Lloyd points out, Great Dixter is more a matter of meticulous planning than of happenstance. Many of the plants—more than a visitor might expect—are hardy, occupying the same position year after year. The Japanese banana, for example, stays in place in the exotic garden right through the winter, protected only with a wrapping of bracken and straw. But the perennial perfection of the displays is also due to a large reserve of plants, grown and kept out of sight until needed. Garrett, according to Lloyd, has perfected a technique of soaking a plant with water a day ahead of time, lifting it and transplanting it to where it is needed, and then soaking it again. "He's got it to a T, so even if [the plant] has been in the open ground, it doesn't notice that it's been moved."

His partnership with Garrett, founded as it is on a shared passion for plants, is the latest evidence of Lloyd's horticultural genius. After seventy-plus years, he can no longer manage Great Dixter alone, but he has turned even that into a source of new vitality for the garden. It is another instance of successful opportunism, one suspects. Just as Lloyd takes his clues from the plants, in this instance he seems to have borrowed a strategy from his beloved dachshunds. As long as anyone can remember there has been a pair of these ferocious guardians on-site—the current couple are named Dahlia and Canna—and the dogs' terrifying attacks have been, traditionally, the high point of any visit. Dahlia, though, is getting old. "She'll be sixteen in December," Lloyd notes. "She used to be quite fierce. But now, she barks and makes the other one do the biting." The approval in Lloyd's voice is unmistakable.

"I want the garden to look as though it's enjoying itself," says Lloyd, who clearly enjoys every day in it himself, even after seven decades.

PART FIVE **INTRODUCTION**

A more plainspoken age might have called these gardens follies. There are those today who still would. Those of us whose definition of a garden begins with plants may be tempted to greet with outrage landscape architect Martha Schwartz's hard-surfaced, flora-free zones. But Schwartz is unimpressed: "I think it is more important to make a place for people than to make a place for a tree." The truth is that a folly is nothing more than gardening to the extreme. It is what a truly exceptional gardener makes when he dares to cross the line. It is where he ends up when he pursues a personal vision past the ordinary limits—to extravagance and sometimes greatness.

Often, the creators themselves are surprised by their journey. Architectural designer Paul Mayén has mocked his own garden as "a monument to my pretentiousness." Actor Tim Curry's great dread, he says, is that the strange and wonderful garden over which he labors will bankrupt him, so that the landscape, never finished, will revert to nature. Martha Schwartz calls herself the "queen of the low-budget jobs" because so many of her designs are improvised (with brilliant ingenuity) from inexpensive, unconventional materials.

PREVIOUS PAGES
According to Paul Mayén, time and thyme are at the heart of this garden walk. Twenty-four varieties of the herb bloom atop the flanking walls.

OPPOSITE
Tim Curry removed forty tons of debris in his quest to revive a lost Hollywood garden, a project as extraordinary as any of his films.

For most of these gardeners, what they do seems to have little to do with choice. It's a compulsion. Bob Clark has made a career out of designing stately landscapes; the wilder, anarchic aspects of his talent could emerge only in his own garden. Once released, they proved unstoppable. For Vietnamese-born Andrew Cao, the act of creation was as much an exorcism as a celebration. Haunted by the lost landscapes of his childhood, he needed to resurrect their beauty. He built the garden for himself because, when he began his practice, he could find no other client.

Those in pursuit of a personal vision work in a long tradition, one with ancient, imperial roots. The gesture that, more than any other, earned the emperor Nero the hatred of his people was not his fiddling while their city burned. It was his seizure afterward of 120-odd acres of downtown Rome so that he could make a country estate in the center of his capital. With its artificial lake and waterfalls, meadows, vineyard, pastures, hunting park, and 120-foot-high statue of the homeowner, the estate became, for Nero, his "Golden House." "Good," he is alleged to have said upon moving in, "now I can at last begin to live like a man." Not for long, though. Within months Nero was dead by his own hand, and his gardens were deliberately destroyed. Nero's successors piously returned the land to public use as a place for baths, streets, and public meeting places—the Coliseum was built on the site of the lake—but they also, one after another, replaced the statue's head with replicas of their own.

Nero's vision was that of a madman, though perhaps that of a mad genius. Given that the only surviving descriptions of the garden were written by his enemies, it's impossible to tell. Other, later follies have survived to prove that they were mad only by contemporary standards. The sacred wood at Bomarzo, Italy, for example, was dismissed as a mere curiosity for centuries, until its "discovery" by Salvador Dalí in 1948. Dalí's enthusiasm arose from the surreal

ABOVE
Andrew Cao calls upon memories of his childhood home in Vietnam to create a symbolic landscape in his Los Angeles backyard.

Martha Schwartz's mirrored wall for the Davis garden in El Paso, Texas, allows everyone who passes through to impose themselves on her design.

power of the monstrous statuary that the garden's creator, a 16th-century count, forced Turkish prisoners to carve out of natural rock outcrops. A recent study, however, by landscape architect Chip Sullivan has also revealed the technical ingenuity of the work, specifically of the climate-controlled cavern where the visitor, by slipping in through a demon's mouth, escapes the heat of the Italian summer.

Times have changed so that today a designer so brilliantly out of step does not have to wait for recognition. In Andrew Cao's case, the garden was considered a great success from the moment of its completion, perhaps because today people are more apt to embrace the eccentric. The English people ridiculed 18th-century architect William Kent when he deliberately transplanted a dead tree to the royal gardens at Kew. (He thought it romantic.) Today, however, we happily pay admission to see trees planted upside down at the Massachusetts Museum of Contemporary Art.

A cynic might ascribe this change to a postmodern world's craving for novelty. There is another, kinder assessment, which undoubtedly comes closer to the mark. Less bound by tradition now, we are less threatened by the unconventional, better able to understand the beauty and strength in it.

Maybe, too, we have learned to admire the courage of those who take a risk. There is a terrible vulnerability that comes with sharing such personal visions. A self-deprecating humor is an almost universal shield among those who do dare. "This sort of Inca pool" is how Tim Curry describes the water feature at the summit of his garden, "a place you sacrifice virgins." Though, he adds, he has not yet done so. Even Martha Schwartz, so brash in her design, is modest in the words she uses about it: "I hope that what I build will make the landscape visible to those who usually don't see it."

Is Schwartz suggesting that her way of seeing will eventually become our way? Surely not. As a professor at Harvard's Graduate School of Design, she is familiar with garden history and knows how difficult it is to mass-market such personal statements. Their strong personality makes them resistant to counterfeiting; by their nature they are not for everyone. Of the experiments he has tried in his own garden, Bob Clark says, "I would never suggest these to clients." Then he adds, "Actually, I would love to do a lot of these for clients, but they would have to become more involved in their gardens."

So we will never see Tim Curry selling sacrificial pools on television, or find Martha Schwartz's garden furnishings at the mall. Having seen their gardens, though, we will see our own differently. The best reason for visiting these places is, of course, to enjoy their eccentric fascinations. They are also inoculations against complacency. After visiting one of them, you're likely to catch yourself looking down the endless American vista of foundation plantings and chemically enhanced turf and wondering which is the folly.

ABOVE

The glass-encrusted structure sparkles with Andrew Cao's memories of his childhood home in Vietnam.

OPPOSITE

In Bob Clark's mixed-media approach to garden design, a water feature combines moisture-loving pond plants with xeriscape favorites such as salvia and lantana. The nearby low wall is studded with an eclectic collection of marbles, pottery shards and pebbles.

PAUL MAYÉN

New York

G ood and bad taste," insisted the late Paul Mayén, "have no meaning for me." He was not boasting; he was just stating a fact. Visit his garden and you will recognize that this prominent architectural designer, who died in 2000, followed his own path. That, in more ways than one, is the strength and the charm of this landscape.

Mayén's roots were in Andalusia, the southernmost region of Spain, and though he emigrated more than seventy years ago, he retained a worldly, cosmopolitan outlook. That, in part, is what sets his garden apart from the neighboring landscapes. After years of teaching architecture and industrial design at New York City's Cooper Union, Mayén chose as his retreat a quiet area well up the Hudson River, in the heart of the country that had been the week-end playground of the nineteenth-century robber barons. But where their follies were ponderous—castles, towers, and other pro-jections of the owners' wealth and power—Mayén's is on a different plane. His extravagances have a lighter touch. The design is very much in the formal tradition, but here, it's all a game. Mayén teased the landscape, wakened the mischief in it. This is a place of elegant promenades and decorum, but they inspire a spring in the step, the hint of a grin on the lips, where pomposity could never take hold. Wherever you wander in this garden, you feel the pres-ence of the owner gently mocking what he described as his own "pretentiousness."

Not that the garden is a joke. Far from it. Mayén had a passion for beauty and grace. The axes of the design are carefully plotted, the elements meticulously related one to another. In a characteristic

OPPOSITE
Mayén described this stone-framed opening to his striped path as a negative pyramid.

flouting of convention, Mayén chose to tuck the house off in a tree-shrouded corner, not inaccessible, but not the focus of the garden, either, as tradition might dictate. Instead, the garden is a world of its own, a fan of paths that radiate from a common point, offering the stroller a choice of experiences and moods. Paths, actually, were the starting point for the design. Paths, after all, are the life force of a garden; they are what carries you along. They were also for Mayén the inspiration, as much an idea as transportation. "When I made a path," Mayén explained, "then I'd start thinking in more traditional terms, like a border."

Where do these paths take you? Perhaps down the "Spanish Walk"—planted with living references to Mayén's birthplace such as *Scilla hispanica*, Spanish lavender, and Iberis, a succession of floral wordplay—to a stone pyramid through which one passes, and then around the obelisk. Finally the path leads into the area Mayén set aside for poetry recitations. Time travel is equally possible; a walk that runs from one stone pyramid to another is edged with earth-filled stone walls, 300-yard-long planters with 24 varieties of flowering thyme. Here, paradoxically, you care about nothing but the moment, should you arrive in late May when the thyme is in bloom.

Alternatively, you can scan the architect's color palette by slipping through the stone-framed triangular gap Mayén called the "negative pyramid," through the white garden, and into the blue spruce room. Not a trip to hurry through, this one, because here the progress is as important as the destination. The walking is easy, but it's important, nevertheless, to watch your feet. If you do, you will notice the path's surface, a grid of honeycombed concrete pavers. These were originally laid as a track for earth-moving equipment brought in for a construction project, but Mayén liked the texture so much he left them in place after the backhoes were gone. Filling the pavers' cavities with gravel gave the resulting walk a smooth surface, but also created a design opportunity.

Mayén used gray gravel throughout, except for a narrow stripe, one paver wide, down the path's center, which he filled with white. Like the center line on a highway, this stripe races forward, not pausing even to avoid the three large rocks Mayén laid down in the path's center. Instead (thanks to a bit of white paint and some careful brushwork) the stripe rushes right over the rocks. Follow the stripe into the room, the opening at the path's end, and up the blue spruce for which this space was named—Mayén pruned away the tree's lower branches to expose the trunk, then painted it white.

The eye is pulled up the tree, then off to a distant hill. Mayén has created a visual one-way street no one can resist.

Balancing the excitement of this room are the quieter pleasures of the garden: the ring of carefully sheared boxwood that hides a mirrorlike pool, the earth's skyward eye, the waterfall and the grotto that furnish an entrance to a hidden tennis court, the statues that watch one another across a path. The pond is busy with herons and kingfishers; it can be seen from the house and gives a clue to what was, surprisingly, Mayén's most acute pleasure. For a man who, seemingly, did nothing by accident, Mayén found his greatest joy in nature's small rebellions—the plant that springs up out of place from a seed deposited by a bird, the tender shoot that against all odds and horticultural wisdom made it through the winter. In spring, the ducks insist on returning while the pond is still frozen, so Mayén slipped out to chop a hole for them in the ice. Life—work, friends, and obligations—kept taking him away, but he never went willingly. "I love it here," he said. "I should be here all the time." In spirit he is.

ABOVE

Blue spruces back a border of blue-flowered Siberian iris and a similarly hued grass, Festuca 'Elijah's Blue.'

A hedge of clipped white pines encloses the area Mayén set aside for poetry readings.

To make sure that the visitor doesn't miss the view of a distant hill, Mayén laid down a stripe of white, carrying it the full length of a path, then up the white-painted trunk of a spruce at the walk's end.

STILES O. CLEMENTS
WITH TIM CURRY
California

With his Emmy Award, Tim Curry probably doesn't miss them, but still you can't help wondering if he has ever taken home from the flower show the silver cups he so obviously deserves. Among all his acclaimed roles, from Dr. Frank N. Furter in *The Rocky Horror Picture Show* to the composer Mozart in the Broadway production of *Amadeus*, Curry's most extraordinary part may be that of the treasure hunter he has played in his own backyard.

When he purchased his Hollywood Hills home, Curry inherited a remarkable garden—or, rather, the site of a once remarkable garden. The house had been built in the 1920s by noted Los Angeles architect Stiles O. Clements. The garden had fanned out and up the slope behind it. By 1993, however, when Curry first saw the 2.2-acre property, it more closely resembled a wildlife preserve. A stag, too sick to be moved, died there soon after Curry moved in; coyotes and raccoons clearly regarded him as an intruder; a number of skunks had to be evicted. The question was, where was the garden? Through decades of neglect, some forty tons of debris had sifted down over the original plantings and paths and terraces, sometimes burying them to a depth of several feet.

Just clearing the ground took six months. Fortunately, Curry was in for the long haul. This English actor claims an affinity for gardening as his birthright. That is what it means to be English. Sometime around age thirty, Curry says, a trowel just appears in your hand. He had already constructed a garden based on the colors of fellow expatriate David Hockney's Mulholland Drive period.

He was looking for a new opportunity, something that could become his horticultural legacy. Our times, Curry explains, are about immediate gratification. In his garden, where he plans for the future, he finds an antidote.

With his long-term perspective, Curry felt that, as well as preparing for the future, his assignment was also to preserve the past. What he began uncovering was classic Californian: a startling mélange of periods and styles that had been stirred together to make a most pleasing, thoroughly theatrical whole.

Just beyond the stagelike terrace that abuts the back of the house was a small, lush, but formal koi and lotus pond; backing that was a Moorish grotto flanked by a bench decorated with tiles that tell the whole action (in Hollywood storyboard fashion) of *Don Quixote*. Water for the grotto spills down the hillside above in a cascade that could have been lifted directly from the Alhambra. Above the cascade is the source of its flow—a rock-enclosed pool that looks, says Curry, like "a place you sacrifice virgins."

On the adjoining terrace he reconstructed the thatched-roof palapa where Fay Wray would have touched up her makeup before the director called the native high priest back from his break and started the cameras rolling again. Curry knew about the palapa because he had seen it in a photograph from a 1925 issue of *House & Garden*; he had searched the ground near the pool until he found the holes that had served as sockets for the original columns so that he could set his reconstruction exactly on the mark.

With the lanterns lit, the pool is romantic enough even without the original cast. "Although it's a bit tiresome coming up here by flashlight," Curry says, "in high summer the night-blooming jasmine is in full flower and it smells like a Turkish brothel, and it's wonderful to swim. You can't see very far, but you can see the lights of the city. Besides, you're guarded by putti," he adds, gesturing at the Victorian stone angels on guard below.

Pulling together a script from so many different stories is not a job for the fainthearted, but Curry has accomplished it with enormous verve. His tool for this has been a self-confident use of plants. He swathed the grotto with climbing roses, festooned an old avocado tree with potato vines, framed the pool with a hundred camellias. He lined the cascade with ribbons of true-blue *Senecio mandraliscae*, punctuating these with red-spiked *Aloe ferox*. He has protected the seventy-year-old palms and the dragon trees, which he hung with Moroccan lamps. He has found space for specimens such as the floss silk tree, spiky crassulas, and a brain cactus

"The idea is organizing nature not just into pleasing shapes, but also as a kind of spiritual resource."

—TIM CURRY

(*Opuntia microdasys*) that looks like a prop from his *Rocky Horror* days. He added his own architectural touches, too, such as a pair of terraces—from the bench on one he can watch the sun rise, while from the bench on the other he can watch it set.

In fact, Curry spends as much of his time here as that arrangement suggests. He is a hands-on gardener who not only plans but prunes and primps himself. The central event of every morning is the inspection of the garden, top to bottom, to see what needs to be done on that day.

That can be almost anything, given the scope of Curry's dreams. Maybe he will add a ziggurat—he could scavenge the base from the concrete fragments of a local road-building project, then decorate it with tiles by Oliver Stone's set designer and tin Venetian canal lamps from the designer of Doris Duke's Hawaiian estate, Shangri-La. Purists may tremble, but the montage that is this garden seems to gather force from the disparate nature of the elements.

There has to be, though, a firm hand and a ruthlessly discriminating eye in command—and Curry lets nothing happen by accident. He may admire the natural sensuality of the god Pan, whose image he has set up to watch over his pond. But he sees himself more as an auteur. Of his Hockney garden, he says, "It was the nearest I'd ever got to being a painter, I think. And probably a sculptor, too." Gardening is his art.

It is also a form of worship. The references you find around his garden—the copper cross from Maine, the cherubim, the Madonnas—are not accidental choices. "The idea is organizing nature not just into pleasing shapes, but also as a kind of spiritual resource, you know? I find it hard to leave this place. If you start gardening and get into it, what you really want is a lifetime garden. And this is, for sure, it."

OPPOSITE
Curry re-created the original thatched palapa from a photograph he found in a 1925 issue of House & Garden.

OVERLEAF
When the night-blooming jasmine is in flower, and the lights of the city are lit, Curry's pool is the perfect place to swim.

ANDREW CAO
California

Inspiration comes from odd sources. Andy Cao found it at the recycling center, uncovering beauty in what others deemed waste. He had emigrated with his family from Vietnam in 1979, but in twenty-five years the memories of his native landscape hadn't dimmed. In some sense, they were still directing his steps. Cao had first studied architecture at the University of Houston, but in 1989, he refocused. Moving to Los Angeles, he enrolled in California Polytechnic Pomona's landscape architecture program. By 1994, he had finished his degree and was ready to act. He had an idea for a garden but no backers. That, ultimately, proved an enormous piece of good fortune.

Andy Cao was thrown back on his own resources, and those turned out to be strangely wonderful. What Cao wanted to do was re-create several childhood scenes. These were not the troubling ones that for a whole generation of Americans are synonymous with Vietnam. Cao, as a native, knew the country better. He knew what a beautiful place it was—or, rather, had been. Cao was determined to bring that back to life. Not surprisingly, no one commissioned the young designer's project. Undeterred, he decided to build it in the 1,500-square-foot backyard that he shared with his partner, Stephen Jerrom, in the neighborhood of Echo Park.

One image in particular had stayed with Cao. He could still see the cones of salt the workers raked up from the brine in Vietnam's coastal salt farms. Crystalline, translucent, the salt glittered in the sun by day and glowed in the moonlight at night. Only glass, Cao decided, could convey the right luminosity.

"When you grow rice, the whole field is like a green carpet."

—ANDREW CAO

With no budget, he began to make the rounds of glass recycling plants, meeting only with rejection until he finally found a plant manager who had been in Vietnam during the war. Cao's project intrigued the man, and he let the young designer pick through the enormous heaps of shards and bottles and take what he wanted. This, it turned out, eventually amounted to some forty-five tons.

Cao had discovered in the glass something much more than a substitute for salt. Made from silica, stuff of the earth, the glass was an appropriate material for making a landscape; ground into chips and balls, it had the jewel-like gleam and the subtle colors of his recollection. In the glass, Cao had found the unifying element for his whole garden.

Cao's theme was Highway 1, the 1,200-mile-long road that connects all the places Cao sought to resurrect: his parents' seaside village in central Vietnam, his grandparents' rice farm in the south, where Cao's family had moved near the war's close, and the terraced paddies of the north. They are all there, now, though, every stop along the way. "When you grow rice," Cao says, "the whole field is like a green carpet. We grew jasmine rice, and every time the wind blew, the whole field smelled of jasmine." Cao caught the flooded paddies in a tufted field of Mexican feather grass that rises out of a ground of cobalt blue glass. He mounded gold and green fragments on black—that is the rice drying on the tarmac. A glass-encrusted boundary wall evokes the coast. But not all is idyllic—a rusted steel sculpture recalls the abandoned armaments that lay beside the highway. And at the back of the garden there is a shallow pool from whose water emerges the cones of white Vietnamese salt reincarnated in a Los Angeles backyard.

The success of this garden is that it achieves far more than an allegorical trip. It has a sense of tranquillity and mystery, of weightlessness as you are buoyed up in the prismatic tide of light. The handful of dramatic plants that Cao chose to include—tropicals such as orchids, gingers, and bananas; the feather grass and various aloes—show off like gems in this setting. They are always changing, and so too, perhaps surprisingly, is the glass. Reflecting

OPPOSITE

Mexican feather grass rising from a crystalline mulch of cobalt blue conjures a remembrance of the flooded paddies.

the light as it does, the glass takes on slightly different hues with every shift in the angle and intensity of the sun. At night, the garden glows as if lit from below.

In the past few years, Cao has used glass to create a prayer garden for Vietnamese-American actress Tiana Alexandra and in a residential project for John Willheim, whose house was designed by John Pawson. He was invited to exhibit his work at the Festival des Jardins, Chaumont-sur-Loire, France, and was awarded a year-long fellowship at the American Academy in Rome. Memories, for Andy Cao, have become visions of the future.

ABOVE
Gold and green mounds recall the heaps of harvested rice drying on Vietnamese highways. Glittering like gems, the glass fragments seem to glow at night.

OPPOSITE
Shifting in hue with every change of sunlight, the blue glass granules supply an intriguing and dramatic backdrop for blossoms of epidendrum orchids.

A rusted sculpture alludes to the armaments that lay abandoned along Vietnam's Highway 1.

BOB CLARK
California

D on't tell my clients how much I like insects," Bob Clark
pleads, almost serious. "And for God's sake, don't tell them
about the opossums."

Clark, after all, has got an image to maintain. He's the man to
call in the San Francisco area if you want a formal garden, and he
does a restrained, cerebral garden very well. He has been the gardener at the Bechtel estate; he replicated an Italian Riviera garden
on a magnificent site overlooking the Bay in Piedmont. But success
has, in one sense, become a trap. There is a sensual and tempestu-
ous side to Clark's imagination that was finding no expression in
his work.

In 1990, he and fellow horticulturist Raul Zumba found a llama
farm back in the hills behind Oakland. It was a stretch to call this
a farm—one acre with a modest ranch house—though the feeding
troughs and stables bore witness to its agricultural use. From
Clark's perspective, the property offered several huge advantages.
There was the rural quality of the neighborhood, the secluded,
sloping site, and, above all, the fact that it could be theirs, his and
Zumba's, to do with as they saw fit.

"I wouldn't call it revenge," says Clark, looking around at what
he and Zumba have perpetrated. "But I have done all the things
my clients wouldn't let me do over the past thirty years." And glorious as the Clark-Zumba garden is, it's risk-taking of a sort that
few gardeners would have the nerve to attempt.

"I wanted a feeling of overwhelming profusion, of profusion
just on the edge of chaos," Clark explains, and the twenty-foot-tall

topiary llama, painstakingly sculpted from Grecian bay, practically
nods in agreement. There is an amazing number of plants packed
into this series of terraces. The house seems to have disappeared,
but it's still there, just buried under the fuchsia and abutilon.
Around it you will find more than a thousand species of flowering
plants, a rainbow of astonishing colors, dozens of sculptures, wild
birds, Baby Baby (the russet bantam rooster that sleeps on the bedroom windowsill), and, of course, the opossums, which the neighbors hate but which Clark and Zumba tolerate because, as Clark
points out, "they eat the snails."

It has been a deliberate policy of Clark and Zumba's to add
much while removing as little as possible. The llama troughs, for
example, were overturned, embellished with bits and pieces found
on the site—fragments of a mirror, old bottles, and light bulbs—
and turned into benches. Zumba incorporated other finds into the
"recycling wall," which he built to shelter the plants from the wind
off San Francisco Bay. Smaller clippings are also recycled, left to
rest wherever they fall so that they revert to humus, along with the
organic debris from the kitchen. The ground here is never raked or
swept: "All we do is blow along the edges of the path."

Plants are also part of the recycling program. Many were trou-
bled or pest-infested specimens written off by clients. "Most people
give up on their plants too soon," Clark says. "Ninety percent of
those we take in survive. We clean them by watering from the top,
a practice I strongly recommend."

Because he is the son of a minister, Clark says he is loath to
preach. Instead, he teaches his organic gardening principles by
example. The outrageous health of the garden is his testament.
"I use a lot of water," Clark says, "but chemicals never." Zumba,
who was raised in Ecuador, says that a similar attitude is part of
his own background: "In South America, we don't even rely on
modern medicine for human illnesses. If a plant is ailing, you don't
immediately think of using chemicals."

The garden is also a laboratory for Clark and Zumba, a place
where they can experiment with plant combinations that violate
the norms. "Right now we are into orange and pink," Clark says,
gesturing to an area where pink-flowered 'Playgirl' roses flirt out-
rageously with the orange 'Playboy' roses, while the rose-blos-
somed *Passiflora jamesonii* carries on a similar sort of affair with a
zonal geranium. Black and chartreuse, Clark says, produce a mysterious brooding effect, as in his partnering of Scotch moss with
black mondo grass, or the deep bronze-purple foliage of *Ajuga*

OPPOSITE
"Profusion just on the edge of chaos"
is his goal, Bob Clark says, and a
twenty-foot llama sculpted from
Grecian bay seems to approve.

> ## "I wanted a feeling of 'overwhelming profusion,' of profusion just on the edge of chaos."
>
> —BOB CLARK

'Metallica Crispa' with the yellow blades of Bowles Golden Grass (*Millium effusum* 'Aureum').

Other plant combinations are less shocking, just unexpected. There is no reason not to mix roses with dry land plants, Clark claims, though no one does. He loves the effect: "The right pink rose with the right gray eucalyptus—if people used their eyes, they would see that the rose, except shrub roses, should never be set out by itself in rows, but always mixed with low plants that hide its ugly branches."

Their appetite for the different is also visible in the collection of artworks that Clark and Zumba have placed among the plantings. These range from a seventeenth-century Ayutthaya Buddha to commissioned pieces from such contemporary artists as Mark Bullwinkle, Michelle Meunig, William Wareham, Marcia Donahue, and Martha Heavenston. Sometimes, fine as the artworks may be, their impact is partly in the display. The grinning metal-face Bullwinkle worked into the front gate, for example, seems delighted with his wild coiffure from a clambering potato vine (*Solanum jasminoides*). Elsewhere, the piquancy lies in the contrast of the plants with department store mannequins, crumbling chalk statues of Miss Piggy, architectural salvage, and a host of found objects.

The unconventional nature of the garden is simply a reflection of the designer. Clark came to California to study economics at Stanford, but discovered after graduation that he couldn't stand to work indoors. He never took a degree in design, just worked his way into it as a gardener, and he is proud of that. "In England," this self-taught scholar notes, "the gardener's vocation includes intellectuals like William Robinson. But here, the gardener is right up there with the dishwasher and the garbageman."

Clark might hate to preach (so he says), but you wonder if it was from his father that he inherited his cosmic concerns. In this garden packed with pleasures and wit, there is also a challenge. "I believe," says Clark, "we can all tolerate more chaos than we think we can. It's a matter of letting ourselves push the limit that separates order and chaos."

Clark is pushing hard.

OPPOSITE
Greeting the visitor at the front gate, this smiling face by artist Mark Bullwinkle warns that inhibitions should be left on the sidewalk.

OVERLEAF
The sunken garden with its peninsula of turf offers an area of repose; "my only rule," says Clark, "is using my eye to determine what goes together."

MARTHA SCHWARTZ

Texas

She is not, says Martha Schwartz, a "nature hater," as some of her critics have charged. She is just a "nature realist." Her landscapes and gardens fascinate many and outrage others, but they almost never leave her audience unmoved. That suits Schwartz. She approaches her work with passion, and her professional goal seems to be to stir it in others.

She succeeded with clients Sam and Anne Davis. They regard the garden Schwartz made for their El Paso home with delight. Schwartz likes delight. But it's not enough by itself. Schwartz wants a garden to play with your perceptions as well, to challenge and make you question assumptions. That is why visiting the Davis garden, like so many of Schwartz's designs, is such a powerful experience. It is simultaneously uplifting, invigorating, and puzzling. Rather like, one visitor has said, "strolling through a candy-colored maze and undergoing shock therapy at the same time."

The shock that this garden delivers comes in part from the tiny role played in it by plants. In this it fits with the rest of Schwartz's work. Her heroes aren't Frederick Law Olmsted and Gertrude Jekyll; in her landscape design she looks rather to the examples of Jasper Johns and Andy Warhol. Schwartz believes that she is working for an urban age. "We live in cities," she has said, "and we can't slather the whole place with so-called nature." Nor does she try. The frogs in a Martha Schwartz garden are most likely to be plastic, and the mulch an assortment of aquarium gravels rather than cedar bark. Too many Americans, Schwartz believes, do not understand that nature has changed. It's no longer a pristine

OPPOSITE
Martha Schwartz summoned up a maze of rooms for her El Paso clients. Here a mound of stone chips punctuates the "Gold Room."

OVERLEAF
A saguaro cactus asserts itself in the "Orange Room"; windows pierced in the wall allow glimpses into other parts of the complex, hints of adventures to come.

wilderness that exists for its own sake; nature is something that, like it or not, exists "only when, where, and how we say it does."

There is undeniable truth in this statement when you consider the suburban habitat in which the Davises, like ever increasing numbers of Americans, live. In the hot, arid outskirts of El Paso, an unsubdued nature wouldn't allow a garden much more than mere survival. The Davises learned that lesson over twenty-five years of trying to coax an English-style border out of desert conditions. Anne Davis, the gardener, wasn't ready to abandon that endeavor, but she did want something different. She showed Schwartz an area between the herbaceous borders and the garage, a walled space thirty-seven feet wide and sixty feet long, what Schwartz has described as "a shoe box."

Schwartz was not discouraged. On the contrary, when Anne Davis set out parameters—low maintenance, a Mexican flavor (El Paso is on the border), with cacti—Schwartz had just the thing. She maintains a double life, as an artist and as a landscape architect, and approaches her design work, by her own admission, "not as a horticulturist or environmentalist," but rather "as an artist." For the Davises she planned a large and intricate piece of sculpture, a series of half a dozen linked spaces within the original wall.

"It's my interpretation of what a Mexican garden means," Schwartz explains. "Mexican gardens tend to be formal, geometric, and spare. The essence of a Mexican garden is the walls. There is a clear definition between public and private, inside and outside."

For Schwartz, working in a Mexican vein was a matter of learning the vernacular rather than copying details. She admired the enthusiastic use of color in Mexico, where "color is used to transform, express, individualize an environment." Accordingly, Schwartz modified her usual Day-Glo palette, something for which she has become famous. Here she alternated between bright hues and somber ones. The exterior walls she painted with "dark, gloomy, almost forbidding colors, which tend to disappear at night." The interior walls she colored pink and orange, like "lanterns that glow."

Schwartz also teaches—she is an adjunct professor at Harvard's Graduate School of Design—and she understands the power of a mental tease. Room leads to room, each one different, with small square windows cut into selected walls to offer glimpses of what is to come. Schwartz gave each room a different character—to each the suggestion of a particular activity.

There's the long, narrow, stall-like bathroom, for example, with

OPPOSITE
In the "Shoe-Box Garden" two cacti suffice for planting. "I think it's more important to make a place for people than to make a place for a tree," Schwartz explains.

chunks of water blue glass crowning its walls; another with a wall studded with threatening nails. The changing room, with its mirrored wall and a crowd of cacti lined up in front of a pink wall, is deliberately unsettling. "It's the idea of vulnerability," Schwartz says. "You are exposed, standing in a bed of cactus." A pair of sculptural saguaro dance a duet in the orange room; in the gold room, a conical pile of stone chips brings a mountain peak from the Rockies down into the shoe box garden, "to make you think about your relationship to it."

Schwartz's brilliance emerges clearly from what was an offhand gesture. Anne Davis wanted to keep her old pool, so Schwartz put it to work. It's the reflecting pond for her garden rooms, a curved sheet of water that twists the image of the articulated walls like a fun house mirror.

There are no plants here, other than cacti, and the visitor has the feeling that even their presence is a concession; Anne Davis specifically requested them. Likewise, the only things in this garden that could be described as wildlife are the sensations and ideas chasing around in the visitor's imagination. That is the game Martha Schwartz pursues. She piles surprise on surprise to keep the visitor off-balance. "It makes the whole less static," she explains. "The idea is to play with your psychology. Gardens are psychological spaces. They take you from your everyday world to someplace else."

ABOVE
Chunks of blue glass atop the walls of the "Bath Room" shine with a submarine light when caught by the sun.

OPPOSITE
Her clients had asked for a Mexican-flavored garden. The Bath Room's glass topping glows like a surreal desert ice.

OVERLEAF
Anne Davis wanted to keep her existing pool; Schwartz turned it into a reflecting pool that captures the image of the new construction.

PART SIX The Cottage
Garden
Reinvented

FEATURED DESIGNERS
IN THIS SECTION:

SARAH RAVEN
England

SARAH AND MONTY DON
England

CHRISTIAN LOUBOUTIN
France

GWENDOLINE AND PETER HAROLD-BARRY
Ireland

PART SIX INTRODUCTION

I t is the most unrepentantly romantic style of garden design, and yet the cottage garden has its roots in pragmatism. What moneyed nostalgia seeks to re-create in a cottage garden is a system of cultivation developed by the rural poor to feed the family. There is a second contradiction: the cottage garden is deliberately simple in style—that's the basis of its appeal. Unless handled with considerable skill, though, a cottage garden slips almost inevitably into the worst kind of sunbonneted sentimentality. In other words, a genuine expression of naïveté demands great sophistication.

Of course, to speak of the cottage garden as a single genre is misleading, because what this term describes is really a provenance rather than a style. Every nation has its own tradition of cottage gardening. As a country of immigrants, the United States hosts many. A little exploration turns up backyard farmsteads of figs, tomato vines, and balsams in our little Italys, the "swept yards" that traveled to the Old South directly from West Africa, and the cheerful but disconcerting marriages of poinsettias and collard greens that one still finds around the cottages of elderly German-Americans in the Texas hill country.

More typically, a reference to cottage gardens summons

visions of thatched roofs and cool-hued perennials—visions, in short, of England. That's fair enough, since it was via England that this folk art worked its influence on the gardens of the carriage trade. The herbaceous border, Gertrude Jekyll's principal gift to garden design, was based, the great lady admitted, on the "pretty tangle" she had found in English cottage gardens. In her appreciation of this motif, Jekyll followed the example of an older colleague and mentor, William Robinson. Though less aesthetically gifted than Jekyll, Robinson was a ferociously combative gardener who once settled an argument with an employer by opening all the windows of the greenhouse in midwinter before leaving the premises forever. Robinson's principal bugaboo, which he pursued through endless articles and books, was the Victorian fashion for "carpet bedding," a paint-by-number technique of marshaling blocks of identical annual flowers into vast, garish representations of the family coat of arms, the flag, or "Welcome to Brighton." As an alternative, Robinson proposed the unself-conscious manner in which the cottagers intermingled diverse plants, thus suggesting and paving the way for Jekyll's innovations.

The cottage style of planting wasn't an aesthetic decision—at least not originally—but rather a matter of economics. In this respect the English cottage garden was identical to that of every other nation and tradition. Its visual appeal was fundamentally a beautiful by-product of an instrument perfectly adapted to its task. For the cottage garden evolved not to please the eye but rather to provide the maximum return in food and other household necessities with the smallest investment of space.

"No cottagers who are wise will ever think of getting a living out of their gardens," warned the editor of *The Cottage Gardener* in the inaugural issue (1848) of this monthly magazine. Only those who might be "contented to live upon nothing but potatoes, cabbages, and similar food" should try this, and even they "would soon

be reduced to the present condition of the Irish peasantry—dragging on at all times a degraded existence, never doing more than just escaping from actual want. No right-minded English cottager will desire such a state of things as this."

Nevertheless, an amazing amount of produce could be extracted from the small space surrounding a rural laborer's house, if properly cultivated. Something like an eighth of an acre was the ideal size, according to the nineteenth-century experts. In such a space, wrote John Claudius Loudon—the early Victorian publisher of *The Gardener's Magazine*—the cottager could cultivate the following: one rod (an area measuring 16.5 feet by 16.5 feet) of onions and leeks, one rod of carrots, one rod of Windsor beans, one rod of parsnips, three rods of cabbages (for a harvest of 525 heads, with a row of scarlet runner beans around the perimeter), four rods of early potatoes, four rods of Prussian potatoes, and six rods of Devonshire potatoes.

Into vacant corners, the cottager might also tuck radishes, peas, early beans, lettuces, cucumbers, gooseberries, cherries, apples, and pears. Space had to be found for a pig, poultry, pigeons, and rabbits, as well as for a tobacco patch. But the planting should not be strictly utilitarian: a man of his times, Loudon insisted that cottagers must also take the opportunity to feed their souls. They must find space in their closely packed plots for appropriately humble flowers such as stocks, carnations, and pinks, as well as for roses and honeysuckles that would drape the house walls.

The themes of beauty and utility emerge from Loudon's instructions. It's doubtful that the original cottagers had the time or energy to carry out such an intensive program, but the insistence on productivity is authentic. Anything like this lengthy list of crops and livestock could only be accommodated by the thriftiest, most ingenious use of space. There simply wasn't room in a cottage garden for the sort of segregation practiced by middle-class or

OPPOSITE
Every land had its cottage gardening tradition; in France, designer Christian Louboutin has re-created the local variant, the jardin de curé.

aristocratic gardeners. Lining plants in well-spaced rows was spatially extravagant; instead, the flowers and vegetables were butted against one another in sheets. Wherever possible, crops were mixed in with other plants, as in the case of Loudon's cabbages and scarlet runner beans. If a spot were vacated at harvest time, something else was immediately planted.

The earliest detailed accounts of English cottage gardens, written in the eighteenth century by approving landlords, reveal that there were always flowers mixed in with the fruits and vegetables. Most often, though, color and fragrance came from the imaginative use of utilitarian plants. The purple-blossomed lavender earned its spot by serving as an insect repellent; its leaves, when scattered among the woolens, warded off moths. A scarlet-blossomed bean had practical as well as aesthetic value. So did the purple-leaved cabbage.

Ironically, it was this practicality that made the cottage gardens so aesthetically powerful. Form followed function. The tightness of the planting made these landscapes irresistibly lush, while the cottagers' talent for finding exceptional beauty in the most common plants endowed their gardens with a surprising elegance. And though necessity has largely disappeared, the best of the contemporary cottage gardens still honor these founding strictures. The tension created by the tight organization of plants still invigorates. It keeps the gardens honest.

OPPOSITE
Contemporary floral designer Sarah Raven finds inspiration, and satisfying harvests, in cottagers' flowers such as these Shirley poppies, a domesticated strain of the corn poppy, an agricultural weed.

SARAH RAVEN
England

It could be argued that Sarah Raven's Perch Hill Farm in East Sussex is a throwback. While taking maternity leave from her work as a physician, Raven began dabbling semiprofessionally in floral design. Dissatisfied with the materials she found available commercially, she began to focus on growing her own, and what began as a professional stopgap turned into a new career as an author, teacher, newspaper columnist, and television personality. Besides serving as a family retreat, her garden is an essential resource for her work. In this sense, it is the modern incarnation of the cottager's plot. It is traditional, though also unique.

Though vegetables remain important in her garden (Raven teaches cooking as well as flower arranging), they take second place to flowers. With their bold, intense hues, the flowers shock as well as please Raven's English clientele. One suspects that this would have pleased her cottage-gardening predecessors. They certainly would have approved of Raven's insistence on cut-and-come-again. Her need for a continual harvest has led Raven to abandon the well-bred gardener's prejudice for perennials and to emphasize in her planting annuals such as dahlias, zinnias, ammi, cleomes, and amaranths. The more you cut these, the more they bloom.

One aspect of her garden that is not traditional—a characteristic it shares with most contemporary cottage gardens—is its size. Raven measures her area not in rods but in acres, and this creates a problem. The original cottagers relied on the constraints of their space to organize the garden and to act as the antidote to an

> "I want to cut it, put it on a plate, and have it taste good; snip it, plunk it in a vase, and have it look good."
>
> —SARAH RAVEN

ad-hoc planting scheme. The architecture of the house, the front walk, and the hedge around the perimeter were sufficient structure for an eighth of an acre. With no more structure than this, however, Raven's Perch Hill Farm would fall into chaos. But the organizational devices that were customarily employed by the cottagers' grander neighbors—axes, pavements, and vistas—would clash stylistically with the cottage garden's intrinsic informality.

The solution came from the other side of the family. Raven's husband, Adam Nicolson, is the grandson of Harold Nicolson and Vita Sackville-West, the creators of England's most famous garden, located at Sissinghurst Castle in Kent. They had confronted the same problem when they began their garden many years earlier. Vita favored romantic abandon in her gardens, but she also treasured the ordered rationality that Harold supplied. The synergistic solution they achieved was to divide the larger space into discrete "rooms" in which the enclosing walls and hedges furnished the sense of order needed as a counterpoint to the floral riots within them.

Raven has adopted this device of "garden rooms," though she has organized her space with a more cottage-suitable combination of low hedges and wattle fences. These dividers achieve the desired result of reducing individual areas to more manageable proportions, but also, in a seeming contradiction, create the impression that the garden as a whole is larger than it really is. The walls transform it into a series of different pleasures and turn what might be a static experience into a progression of emotions and sensations.

OPPOSITE

Building on the cottagers' theme of productivity, Raven favors cut-and-come-again flowers such as these 'Requiem' and 'Red Velvet' dahlias.

ABOVE
The child-friendly simplicity of the cottage style is important to Raven, for whom motherhood was the original entrée into a horticultural career.

LEFT
Raven uses low hedges and wattle fences to organize her garden space.

OVERLEAF
Raven's emphasis on annuals such as this carpet of orange calendulas, blue bachelor buttons, and purple Salvia viridis *runs counter to fashionable gardening practice, but is true to the cottage-garden tradition.*

SARAH AND MONTY DON
England

When a style loses its ability to surprise, it also loses its vitality. To let the cottage garden die in this fashion would be especially inopportune. Although cottagers of the original sort may be facing extinction, commuters and weekenders are not, and the cottage garden is in many respects ideally suited to this new generation's schedule. After all, the unstudied tousle of the cottage garden looks most appealing when slightly neglected, which means that a cottage garden is typically closest to perfection when the owner pulls into the driveway on Friday evening. By Sunday night, after a weekend of weeding and clipping, the same garden is likely to have the uneasy composure of a teenager's hair wetted and combed into place before a date. At that very moment, however, the contemporary gardener bids it good-bye and the garden will have recovered its élan by the following Friday.

Another timely feature of this old-fashioned style of gardening is that it lends itself to the contemporary desire for a more environmentally friendly type of maintenance. Having evolved before the invention of synthetic chemicals, traditional cottage-garden plants typically offer an outstanding resistance to pests and diseases. And if a particular species should succumb, the patchwork and informal character of cottage-garden planting ensures that this loss doesn't leave a large or obvious gap. Nor are pollution-belching power tools essential to the maintenance of a cottage garden. On the contrary, the clean-shaven profile produced by gas mowers, string trimmers, and shears do not harmonize with a cottage-garden setting.

OPPOSITE
Jewelry designers Monty and Sarah Don have created a lapidary masterpiece in their garden and remade themselves into garden authorities of celebrity stature.

Sarah Don's multifaceted "Jewel Garden" mixes herbs, vegetables, and flowers. By softening the edges, she intentionally blurs the transition from garden to countryside.

Still, timely as the cottage-garden style may be, the question remains: What can be added to this aesthetic? At least one contemporary example, which can be found in Monty and Sarah Don's Jewel Garden in Herefordshire, England, suggests that the future of the cottage garden is indeed bright. The Dons, after all, are authorities on "brights." Monty, the more public member of the couple, is known for his garden columns in The Observer and as the host of a BBC gardening program; he has also made his name as one of the annual television commentators for the Chelsea Flower Show. To the surprise of many, however, he began his career as a costume-jewelry designer in partnership with his wife. The arrangements of "brights" (costume gems) that the Dons sold from their store in Knightsbridge, London, throughout the 1980s attracted clients such as the late Princess Diana. When they moved to the country in 1992, their medium changed, but not their art.

They are still stringing together sparkling bits of color. While the house they purchased had lots of history—it had a Tudor core, seventeenth-century barns, and an early nineteenth-century hops kiln—it had no gardens. So they began the process of constructing a garden by reducing the space to a grid, with intersections of espaliered lindens, broad walks, and narrowed gravel paths that framed a total of sixteen beds. Into each of these beds they injected intense colors—no pastels—and played the flowers and foliage off one another so that the resulting garden pulsates with energy. Inky blossoms of *Centaurea cyanus* 'Black Ball' and the chocolate flowers of *Cosmos atrosanguineus* are played against the lime-green foliage of honey locust 'Frisia' and *Rubus cockburnianus* 'Golden Veil.' Sapphire flowers of monkshood (*Aconitum* 'Henry Sparkes,') glow in a setting of golden *Ligularia dentata* 'Desdemona.' The magenta of *Geranium* 'Ann Folkard' draws an unaccustomed drama from its juxtaposition with the yellow of French marigolds.

These are uncommon colors used in startling ways; they are certainly not the traditional fare of the old-time cottagers. But the Dons' focus on details and visual saturation is certainly authentic. "The garden is quite intensely put together, with saturated spaces of color," says Monty Don, "but there's always an escape route. You turn your head and you see a path that leads out to the countryside." And the countryside, after all, is the place where the cottage garden was born and where, when it is doing its job, it takes us still.

OPPOSITE

Chocolate-flowered Cosmos atrosanguineus *rises from a froth of* Deschampsia cespitosa *'Golden Dew'; the Dons have become famous for uncommon colors used in startling ways.*

ABOVE

Daughter Freya Don wears one of the costume jewelry necklaces that first made the Dons famous in the 1980s.

LEFT

The 19th-century hop kiln (at rear) has become the Dons' office and a vantage point from which to survey the garden.

SARAH AND MONTY DON • 389

CHRISTIAN LOUBOUTIN

France

Besides the obvious themes of self-sufficiency and thrift, the aristocratic advocates of the cottage garden in eighteenth- and nineteenth-century England also promoted them as a source of spiritual uplift. A letter published in *The Gardener's Magazine* in April 1826 was entitled "On the Benefits to be Derived by the Country Labourer from a Garden." The correspondent agreed that the initial purpose of encouraging this activity was "to draw off a peasant from the alehouse," but that by obliging the new gardener to plan and schedule, it would also teach the "gratification [of a] mental pursuit." By introducing beauty in the form of flowers, "we have now got our peasant one degree above mere profit and animal gratification."

The correspondent went further in describing what he termed "An Interesting Scene"—the awarding of prizes by one Andrew Johnstone, Esq., to the best cottage gardeners of his Halesworth estate. In what was clearly meant to be a heartwarming recitation, the reader encounters boys posting banners that read God Speed the Spade and Long Live the Kind Giver while Mr. Johnstone delivers "useful remarks" on the desirable moral and religious conduct for tenants. After reading a passage from the Bible, Johnstone leads the audience in a singing of the doxology and then distributes meat pies.

One can guess what the cottage garden might have become in a less earnest atmosphere by viewing Christian Louboutin's spectacular creation at Champgillon, in the Vendée region of western France. The setting here is decidedly undemocratic, the grounds of

OPPOSITE
Having made a career in fashion design, Christian Louboutin knows all about peacocks; at home in Champgillon, he is a collector of ornamental fowl.

OVERLEAF
The iris allée, reaching northward from the main house, is a particularly beautiful piece of the puzzle Louboutin has assembled on the château grounds.

"Planning a garden is a mystery to be solved, a series of clues to be unlocked."

—CHRISTIAN LOUBOUTIN

a 13th-century château. What Louboutin has created is appropriately elegant: It draws clearly on his sense of style as a fashion designer, but it is firmly in the tradition of the more upscale branch of the French cottage garden than the English version. What Louboutin created, arguably, is the apotheosis of the *jardin de curé*.

This is the name used by the French when describing a sort of garden modeled on those maintained in the past by the small-town and rural parish priests. They are the nearest things that France's horticultural tradition offers to the cottage gardens on her side of the channel. A *jardin de curé* shares the compact scale of the English cottage garden. The curé was not a peasant, nor was he a wealthy man. Generally, he cultivated the fashion of Candide—by himself. To a large extent, these priests shared the cottagers' pragmatic goals: they wanted vegetables for the pot, and herbs for culinary and medical use, since visiting the sick was part of the curé's pastoral duties.

Not all was earthly practicality in the priests' gardens; flowers were included not just for personal gratification but also as a source of spiritual inspiration. Still, like the cottager, the curé favored plants that combined utilitarian as well as aesthetic rewards, and he did not scruple to combine the decorative with the useful. In fact, the decorative French kitchen garden, the potager, is said to derive in part from the priests' gardens. The priests themselves were conscious of their place in a tradition, and they drew on the traditions of the monastic garden in laying out their own, which also set them apart from the gardens of peasant cottagers. Though the curé might intermingle plants informally in cottage-garden style, he typically organized the space like a medieval cloister garden, using perpendicularly crossed paths to divide the planting area into a four-square of symmetrical beds.

By his own account, the Parisian-bred Louboutin is no horticultural scholar. He recalls loathing the countryside whenever his work in fashion design first took him to the provinces. The noise of the insects and birds kept him awake at night: "I was petrified of nature. I couldn't stand it." He took up garden-making only after joining his friend Bruno Chambelland in an effort to restore the Chambelland family home in the Vendée. Chambelland assumed responsibility for the interior restoration and left the out-of-doors job to Louboutin. The latter's talent as a designer had an obvious

relevance to this work, but for the rest, he ascribes his success to a
fondness for puzzles. They had been his hobby as a teenager, and
he found the analytical skills they required identical to those
required in the working out of landscape problems: "Planning a
garden is a mystery to be solved, a series of clues to be unlocked.
For instance, if you do a square allée, you don't just see the outside, you must see the inside. You discover. In a garden, like a puzzle, you discover things from every side. It's a balance of seeing
something that has been done by nature and something that has
been done by you."

Louboutin was greatly influenced by the writings of Vita
Sackville-West, and if his gardening has been carried out on a scale
far grander and more elegant than even that of the jardin de curé,
nevertheless it preserves much of the flavor of a cottage garden writ
large. There is the lush déshabillé style of his iris allée, the tumult
of color in the beds. Louboutin's garden is as full of scratching fowl
as a cottager's, but naturally he maintains the ornamental breeds
of chickens rather than the fryers or layers.

Louboutin takes refuge in the conservatory in winter. "It's most wonderful when it is snowing," he explains.

GWENDOLINE AND PETER HAROLD-BARRY
Ireland

An enhanced scale and an affluent style have become common to many contemporary cottage gardens. The program that had been aimed at the redemption of the working class has ended with the conversion of the upper crust.

This was a result of a demographic shift that occurred throughout Great Britain and much of the rest of northern Europe. Those whom Victorian reformers had hoped to reach with their gardening programs—agricultural laborers and the rural working poor—were already a vanishing species by the second half of the nineteenth century. Their disappearance from the countryside, oddly enough, raised the remaining cottagers' social status. Whereas formerly they had been regarded as an object for improvement, the cottagers now became objects of nostalgia. The poor, as is so often the case, proved far more picturesque in retrospect.

As authentic cottage gardens became a rarity, the remaining specimens acquired the cachet of antiques. In particular, they became a favorite subject for a generation of late-Victorian English watercolorists such as Birket Foster and Helen Allingham, who filled their gardens with pink-cheeked children and rambling roses, and purged them of the smell of the privy and hog. Thanks to Gertrude Jekyll and William Robinson, upper-class gardeners had already absorbed elements of the cottagers' style of planting; now many began to collect cottage gardeners' plants, finding space on their estates for the heirloom pinks and roses, much as a contemporary stockbroker might use an old cobbler's bench as a coffee table in her suburban living room.

OPPOSITE
A place of dreamy peace, this lush pond-side planting was inspired by a painting by Henri Rousseau.

This was not all to the bad. In the right hands, these cottage garden revivals on the grand scale could rise above the inherent mawkishness to become a powerful, if dreamily romantic, vision of an arcadian past—a past all the more appealing for the fact that it never existed. Indeed, this vision of the benevolent garden lost is the definition of paradise in the Judeo-Christian tradition. When coupled with a virtually subtropical climate, as it has been at Creagh, on the coast of Ireland's County Cork, the result can be as convincing as Scripture.

The gardens at Creagh are an anachronism in their own right. The house, built in 1820 during the heyday of the English regime in Ireland, is a fair example of an Anglo-Irish Ascendancy residence. The gardens, however, date only to 1945 and were begun by the then owners, the Harold-Barrys, a full generation after the power of the landlord class had been finally shattered by Irish independence.

This may explain the richness of the landscape, which combines standard aristocratic artifacts—a serpentine pond, a folly, and a walled kitchen garden—with a replica of a Congolese thatch and plaster hut, and the unaristocratically lush planting. Space was made for a cottage garden filled with lupines and delphiniums, an herb garden, and a small, elegant palace for poultry. This hybrid landscape retains its power, too.

The Harold-Barry graves may be overgrown, since, like most Anglican churches in Ireland, the one at Creagh has been long since abandoned and deconsecrated, and its churchyard is reverting to wilderness. The current owners, who apparently find the gardens just as relevant to their lives as had the vanished Ascendants, meticulously maintain these treasured domains.

OPPOSITE
An exotic note is struck by the thatched Congolese hut; near to it stands a red-flowered telopea tree, one of the few specimens outside its native Australia.

LEFT

High walls protect Creagh's herb garden and the newly restored 1940s-era greenhouse.

OVERLEAF

Creagh nurtures a subtropical flora of palms, tree ferns, and New Zealand flax warmed by the Gulf Stream. The owners' rejection of chemical pesticides makes the garden a haven for badgers, butterflies, and nightingales.

THE NEW MODERNISM

PART SEVEN INTRODUCTION

American modernism was born in California in the 1930s, and today it is being born there again. Not that California gardeners are conscious of their leadership. They publish no manifestos, host no joint exhibitions. There is little evidence even that the various leaders of a new modern movement are particularly conscious of one another's work. Nonetheless, they are subtly redefining our relationship to the landscape.

Nature in their hands is becoming less natural, though far more eloquent. That is not to disparage the horticultural craftsmanship of these designers. Typically, it is impeccable. Most of the new modernists are deeply interested in how plants grow. Ron Herman grew up working in the nursery trade; Roger Warner has described himself as an adolescent "orchid geek"—raising orchids "when by rights I should have been cruising in my Chevy." Isabelle Greene, a passionate botanist since childhood, not only possesses a thorough knowledge of the flora of her state but can explain in detail why various plants grow naturally where they do. Topher Delaney was a latecomer in this respect, moving into landscape architecture from previous studies in philosophy and cultural anthropology. As a designer she has developed a deep and informed appreciation of the

natural ecology of a site, and this is expressed in her planting, albeit through the filter of an artist's re-imagining.

Thanks to their horticultural and environmental expertise, these designers' gardens work quite well on a practical level, all the while defying the traditional gardener's view of plants. There are no "specimens" in the neo-modernist garden, nor are there companion plants, or naturalistic evocations of wild plant communities. There seems, instead, to be an effort to appreciate each plant not for how it may be useful, but for its intrinsic strength and beauty. As such, plants become abstract elements in abstract designs that are sometimes disconcerting and always powerfully evocative.

Iconoclastic as these gardens may be, they spring from a tradition of their own, and to understand the achievement of the current crop of California prodigies, it is essential to understand where and how the modernist garden originated.

ABOVE

Hidden lighting endows this Topher Delaney courtyard with a mysterious glow.

A collision with the fine arts was the catalyst for the emergence of a group of gardeners as familiar with the palette knife as the trowel. Paris, in the first decades of the twentieth century, was the locus. Fauvists, cubists, and surrealists had taught their patrons to see the world differently, and the more consistent among them began applying this new vision to every aspect of their lives. As early as 1912, a "Maison Cubiste" was presented at the Salon d'Automne, and within a decade architectural pioneers such as Le Corbusier were turning such conceptual work into bricks and mortar, glass and steel. Structures of such an uncompromisingly new character clearly demanded a different sort of setting, and a variety of artists and architects began dabbling in landscapes suited to the new sensibility.

The results ranged from the brilliant to the bizarre: plazas shaded by concrete trees, pools afloat with ten-foot-wide artificial flowers, a vicomte's villa with a garden designed as a masonry grid, a Chinese checkerboard into whose squares one dropped (or pulled) flowers at will. No longer was planting carried out in imitation of nature or as an expression of aesthetic principles. Instead, it had become a tool for working directly on the imagination and emotions of the visitor.

Not surprisingly, the market for such gardens remained limited, and modernism would almost surely have remained a footnote in the history of garden design if its seeds had not been transplanted to more welcoming soil. Thomas Church, a graduate student at Harvard's School of Landscape Architecture, heard reports of this new modernism and took the ideas with him in 1929 when he returned home to California.

Church found there the most breathtaking possibilities when he set up practice in the 1930s. Lounging amid the palms and lawns today, it's easy to forget just how artificial the contemporary landscape of California is. Before the construction of the dams and aqueducts, most of what is now lush suburb was semidesert. California, in the coastal belt that hosts the population centers, is man-made and, at least at the residential level, it was the landscape architects who invented it. Many were involved in this process, but no one more so than Thomas Church. By the time of his death in 1978, his style—modernism adapted for the masses—had come to define "California style." He is still the one against whom the new modernists measure themselves, and against whom they react.

Church's genius was to understand something that still drives modernist design in California: a man-made landscape practically demands an artificial treatment. Church was fortunate in finding, in California's post–World War II building boom, a clientele not only ready to break with the past, but intent upon doing so. He aimed his business at the middle class that was pouring into the new suburbs, where he found clients who had never had a garden before and so had no preconceptions to cramp his style. Church's clients likely had never heard of Joan Miró or Jean Arp (Church's favorite artists), but they let him create for them outdoor living spaces designed along the same striking, crisp, clearly artificial lines.

Church completed the plans for an incredible 2,000 gardens over the course of his career, and his focus on the interpenetration of house and garden at the very least facilitated contemporary California's indoor-outdoor lifestyle. The "maintenance-free" materials that Church embraced—concrete, asphalt, and rolled gravel (the time had come, he explained, "when it was easier to get a janitor than a gardener")—continue to be an important part of the California modernist's vocabulary.

The patrons of the new modernism tend to be highly educated; their desire for a new kind of garden often springs from their experience with the other arts. Mia Lehrer didn't design jazz musician Lee Ritenour's garden; she composed it. Ron Herman's clientele comes to him in part because they know and share his grounding in

the classical culture of Japan. Roger Warner made his name as a designer with the gardens he designed for a couple of patrons of the San Francisco Museum of Modern Art. "Tommy Church," Roger Warner insists while describing that commission, "wasn't in my head." That could be, for Warner is a genuinely original, largely self-taught talent. But if Church wasn't in Warner's head, he may well have been in those of Warner's clients.

Church's success had the effect of turning iconoclast into icon, transforming his modernism into the old modernism. What is new about today's modernism is in part its reassessment of Church's style. His contemporaries regarded Church's work as an escape from the past; the new modernists, by contrast, find in it a traditionalist strain. Their comfort with that shows how they are redefining their own art. "A lot of Church's design was very formal and classical," says Ron Herman, "but then he twisted that. It's a surreptitious use of tradition." The same could be said of the Japanese concepts that underlie much of Herman's design, or of Warner's admission (again, half joking) that the designer who inspired him most was Capability Brown.

New modernists are also twisting the modernist tradition. Their more intimate acquaintance with plants and the hands-on side of gardening makes their work notably warmer and more inviting. Church tended to hard surfaces and edges, which gave to the best of his work a clean and graceful graphic elegance, but it also made his gardens spaces you might admire but were not likely to want to linger in. That, certainly, is not the case with Mia Lehrer's jazzy, exuberant explosions—you can't bear to leave the party. Unless, perhaps, to retire to the soft, disciplined comfort of an Isabelle Greene garden, the cerebral passion of a Ron Herman design, or the elegant expressiveness of a Roger Warner landscape. Different visions all, different Californias that all, somehow, ring true. And why not? This is the state of reinvention, the place where anything is still possible.

Though an expert in the ecology of her territory, designer Isabelle Greene likes to create what she calls "museumlike arrangements." Her plantings are abstracted, not copied, from nature.

ISABELLE GREENE
California

f there is a quintessence of California comfort and laid-back
ease, it must be Santa Barbara. The climate here is so seductive
it can be debilitating. There's an antidote at hand, however. If
you truly understand the circumstances, and Isabelle Greene does,
you can look right past the imported lawns and palms and see the
discipline inherent in the dry, rocky landscape beneath. Isabelle
Greene sees that, and she made it the heart of the garden she
designed for a client and friend.

Greene is deservedly famous for working with the land. Where
an earlier generation of California landscape architects typically
began a job with a bulldozer, remodeling the site according to their
own vision, Greene prefers to transform through enhancement
rather than imposition. "I have a natural desire to use what's
there," Greene explains. "It works as a rudder on the imagination
and produces a much richer, much more developed design."

In fact, this garden could not be more lush—in an austere sort
of way. Stepping down the hillside in a series of neatly inset terraces, it has taken the natural contours as its own. Photographs of
Balinese rice paddies, Greene says, were an inspiration; she loves
the organic way in which they merge the man-made with the
mountains. But she also drew on lessons she has learned closer to
home, flying back and forth across the United States. She loves to
look out the window of an airplane because, she says, "it turns the
landscape into patterns." She adds that "the whole business of
what things really are gets transformed into these curious images.
I love to reinterpret those and put them into the garden."

OPPOSITE
*The idea of water, rather than water
itself, plays a central role in this
Isabelle Greene garden. Here a
silvery pool of snow-in-summer seems
to feed adjacent beds of lavender,
candytuft, and Shasta daisies.*

So Greene gave this garden her own aerial view. The designer sculpted terraces with earth-toned concrete poured into forms made of split cedar shakes to give it a natural texture, then, taking a central space, she sliced it on the bias with wooden header boards into a strongly geometrical but irregular puzzle. The owner alters her "crops" at will, substituting, say, kale for marigolds, so that her garden constantly changes while still remaining the same.

"What appeared in her garden were farmlands," Greene says. "I like the stripes you look down on from a plane. There may be a stripe of mowed wheat, which is a subtle brownish color, and then a stripe of the wheat that has been harvested—it's a bright golden color. Then the brown again, then the golden. They dead-end, maybe irregularly, at a creek that crosses the land there. On the other side of the creek, another farmer may have stripes going in another direction."

The choice of a flora is hardly arbitrary, at least not for the garden as a whole. Botany is a subject Greene has been studying ever since she was a child in Pasadena. Before the age of ten, she was pressing specimens of native wildflowers, and as a teenager she filled her bedroom with specimens of minerals and mushrooms preserved in jars of formaldehyde. Botany became her major at UCLA because it promised the most time out of doors, though she coupled this with explorations of geology, geography, and climate so that she could begin to understand the whole ecology of her state. "It became very solid in my mind why something grows here, why [as a manipulator of the landscape] you can do this and you can't do that."

Not surprisingly, Isabelle Greene's gardens are famous to a great extent because they work. Like this garden, they fit their setting so well that they flourish with a minimum of care. Rainfall in Santa Barbara is just over 16 inches a year and the city suffers from a chronic water shortage, so Greene lavished the site with drought-resistant plants, with only an occasional accent of some thirstier planting such as the espaliered apple fence at the garden's foot.

Greene's characteristic palette is that of her native southern California, the softly elegant gray-greens, tans, ochers, and silvers that clothe the coastal hills. The individual plants, however, are often not from California; Greene is not dogmatic in that respect. Here, Mediterranean herbs—lavender and rosemaries—mingle easily with desert agaves, aloes, and candytuft. Shade for the arbor is furnished by a giant Burmese honeysuckle. While not technically native to California, these plants are all, thanks to Greene's ecological insight, at home, and the effect is to give a regional flavor even

OPPOSITE
While evoking the impression of water, Greene acknowledges the reality of this landscape in her drought-resistant planting, here a mix of agaves and senecios.

OVERLEAF
Greene loves flying because when you look down the rural landscape is turned into patterns. She has evoked such an agricultural vista in this garden.

to her most abstract work. Arguably, Greene is the most purely abstract of California's contemporary designers because her work derives not from human examples, primarily, but rather from a sort of applied science. "I have a great desire not only to simplify and hone the designs but also to better express the huge natural systems a landscape rests on: the watersheds, plant and animal migrations, the weather, the soil."

Because of its scarcity, water plays a central part in this landscape—not actual water, for the most part, but rather the impression of it. There is a small pool just inside the gate by which visitors enter, but the stream that drains from this is just a twist of blue-gray gravel, inlaid into a pavement of tawny crushed rock. It runs as a river through its floodplain to the plunging dry-gravel "water path" that bounds the garden's flank. As you walk dry-shod along the path that finds its way across the terrace through sterling fields of snow-in-summer and *Senecio serpens*, you feel that you are negotiating another riverine ghost, a cool meander of the imagination.

Paradoxically, this mistress of the abstract is also wary of losing touch with hands-on reality. She is particularly impatient with the modernist tradition of inscribing a painterly graphic line. "Drawing a plan," she observes, "you can get out your little templates and your compass, and you can make curves and straight lines and squares and things. It's something that looks pretty good in graphite on paper on the desk. But that's totally out of context. Only when these things are blown up life-scale and put on the ground do you actually have a plan. But I don't think it always works that way."

It didn't in this garden, at any rate: moods shaped the spaces. There's the meditative, Zen-like calm of the entrance area with its pool; the intimacy of the little kitchen garden with its potted herbs; the lush fertility of the farm-inspired terraces below and the omniscience of the view from above.

This plan did not come from any pencil. It came, Greene says, from time spent alone, consulting the site. "And I don't know how much time it will take," she adds. "Then I just do whatever I need to do to feel embraced by the space—I wander around, go exploring things, actually become a little child and I wait for things to happen … I just patiently wait." She waits for sensations—of height, of depth, of heat and light or shade. Ultimately, the site gives her a direction. "There's always a kind of a rush that becomes the core, the theme, the idea that carries all the way through to the end of the job."

The uncompromising geometry of the house caused Greene to counter with a geometry of her own: rectangular beds stepping down, their edges softened by the cascade of plants.

The sculpture by Anne Hirondelle and the mottled spheres of Kathleen Hanna give focus to a contemplative corner. The ribbon of gray gravel runs through the tawny pebbled bed like a California river viewed from a serene height.

MIA LEHRER

California

There is a definite Latina flair to her gardens. A native of El
Salvador, Mia Lehrer feels that life is to be lived outdoors,
that elegance can dance. There are different steps, naturally,
for different clients. Two art collectors needed something spare and
precise to suit the geometric simplicity of the house that Riccardo
Legorreta was building for them. Jazz musician Lee Ritenour needed
a bit of syncopation and swing for his home in Malibu. In either
case, though, Lehrer's object is the same: "I want to pull people out
into the garden."

Whatever it takes to connect, she will use. The art collectors
ran out of gallery space indoors, so she persuaded them to move a
Henry Moore sculpture into the garden, to start an outdoor collection. She experimented with tropical plantings, gingers and philo-
dendrons, different palms, creating her own sculptural effects by
displaying the bold-leaved plants in isolated groups. For Ritenour,
Lehrer also learned how to express her design in his particular
idiom. The bond between client and architect was strong and immediate. Lehrer's mother was Brazilian, so she connected instantly
with the musician's Brazilian-inflected music. She immersed herself
in it while she worked on his design, and found its vocabulary the
ideal means of communication. Plants and architectural elements
came to function as notes and chords, assembling themselves into
musical tropes. Lehrer cites the "rhythm of the double palms
running the length of the house, the circles like notes going from
the front of the house to the studio area." Even the architectural
elements play along here—a flight of four steps at the head of a

OPPOSITE
*The flamboyant tropicals Mia Lehrer
chose for this garden provided the
perfect complement for the simple
lines of the Ricardo Legorreta house.*

"I want to pull people out into the garden."

—MIA LEHRER

terrace sways in a samba, while the edge of the nearby swimming pool picks up and restates the theme.

Erasing the lines between different arts has been a characteristic of modernism from the beginning; working in abstractions, the designer communicates rhythms and harmonies as easily in musical phrases as in colors or textures. Lehrer avoids the chilliness that could come with such a cerebral approach by her love of both craftsmanship and plants.

The former she attributes to the powerful influence of Salvadoran culture, which has an ingrained admiration for craftsmanship of any kind, and to her father, a salesman of building supplies who used to take her out to building sites when she was a child. Whatever the inspiration, Lehrer is remarkable for the beauty she finds in the plainest industrial materials. She fashioned the Ritenour terrace, for example, from simple concrete slabs, staining them with various pigments and dropping them into the lawn like horizontal paneling. She paved the entrance to the collectors' house in a whirl of irregular Kenesaw stone blocks, provoking a dialogue between house and landscape.

Her interest in plants is visceral, wide-ranging, and shaped by her immigrant experience. She likes learning languages and speaks several; she also knows how to ground herself quickly wherever she ends up. She goes to local nurseries to see what the gardeners are using, and then drives around the town to check what's growing well and how it is being used.

Quoting the late Roberto Burle Marx (another Brazilian connection and a friend), Lehrer says that with planting "you don't do one or two of anything. You do one hundred, two hundred." You wield a broad brush, and you paint with assurance.

This, she says, is part of what distinguishes her work from that of an earlier generation of modernists. She admires the austerity of their work. "I love to look at those gardens," she acknowledges, "but I probably couldn't discipline myself to keep them that way." Nor, she thinks, could her clients. Her experience has taught her that people's relationship to their gardens has changed in the last half-century. Where Thomas Church sought the means to free his clients from gardening, Lehrer finds that hers want to be involved.

OPPOSITE
Viewed from the spa, the columnar trunks of queen and washingtonia palms give a rhythm to this terrace at a back corner of musician Lee Ritenour's house.

OVERLEAF
Steps move from pool to terrace with a samba-like rhythm; Lehrer connected immediately with client Ritenour's Brazilian-inflected jazz.

RON HERMAN

California

T he synthesis is the new." There's a koanlike resonance to
Ron Herman's assertion, and no wonder, for Herman has
devoted a large part of his professional life to the understanding of Japanese design. One of the San Francisco Bay Area's
foremost landscape architects, Herman has made Japan, and in
particular Kyoto, a second home. But what he has found in Japan's
classic gardens he has used to break new ground in California. He
synthesizes. He draws on a portfolio of techniques gathered from
Japanese tradition, applying them with a contemporary understanding to achieve landscapes that are astoundingly fresh.

That Herman should have come to work for software magnate
Larry Ellison seems fated. Ellison shares Herman's appetite for
innovation, as well his fascination with Japanese culture. Ellison
takes personal inspiration from a sixteenth-century samurai,
Miyamoto Musashi, who wrote poems when he was not gaining
fame as a warrior. Ellison had already retained Herman to help
him complete an earlier project—an elaborate water and stroll garden at his Silicon Valley home. This new commission at Ellison's
Pacific Heights town house, however, presented a quite different
challenge: to create a garden in a small entry court and a sharply
sloped courtyard in the center of the house. Complicating matters
even further was the computer-age architecture of the stainless-
steel-and-glass house.

Herman recognized in this an outstanding opportunity, for
landscape design on the crowded Japanese islands has always been
about expanding the possibilities of small spaces. The minimalist

"…the path to modernity is through the past."

—RON HERMAN

elegance of the traditional Japanese style would harmonize comfortably with the microchip aspect of the building.

Herman's father was a Hollywood nurseryman and landscape contractor, and helping with the family business exposed Herman to two very different cultures. On the one hand, there were his father's clients, the movie and television people; on the other, Herman's fellow workers, who included a disproportionate number of first-generation Japanese immigrants, or nisei.

From the first group, Herman absorbed a respect for stage-craft—not a bad preparation for his future career, since, as Herman notes, a lot of California architects learned their business in set design. Meanwhile, Herman was absorbing an interest in the culture of his fellow workers, an interest that would take him, after completing his degree in landscape architecture at Berkeley, to pursue advanced studies at Kyoto University. He has continued to follow the dual path, teaching at Berkeley and practicing in California with time off for three more academic fellowships in Japan.

In the design of Ellison's new garden, he began with the decision that the space should be in the Zen tradition, an object for contemplation rather than the center of activity that Western gardens more commonly become. The frame, however, would employ the latest materials and technologies in an almost cinematic manner to create what amounted to a series of screens with controlled views—but views with a puzzling ambiguity. A steel-framed slot in the front entry court wall provides the first glimpse, a vertical peek into the garden. Inside, glass panels enclose an adjoining gallery and embrace a circular staircase, permitting garden views from various points within the house. The glass panels wrap the courtyard in reflective surfaces to duplicate and shuffle the images. Herman also sheeted water across polished stone surfaces, even degassing the water first to eliminate bubbles and make the mirror more perfect.

Nature doesn't seem to follow the ordinary rules here. A huge rock, a rough basin into which water trickles, hangs in midair, suspended from a steel cable; limestone paving runs across the courtyard, up a wall, spilling into the house, merging interior and

OPPOSITE
Suspended from a steel cable, the massive stone basin hovers, seemingly weightless, above a bed of dwarf mondo grass.

exterior space. Squares of baby's tears alternate with squares of black Mexican river cobbles in a staggered cascade down an incline. Only three species of plant have been admitted: baby's tears, bamboo, and mondo grass, but the plants are all the more prominent for the sense of restraint. Posed like sculpture, reproduced endlessly in the reflective surfaces around them, the plants take on the quality of icons, turning this urban space into a nature spirit's uncanny shrine.

With so few elements, Herman says, the emphasis had to be on the meticulous craftsmanship of each. The courtyard floor, for example, is inset with a bronze grid, in an evocation of the modular system of Japanese building, which erases the distinction of house and garden by laying both out in rectangular units equal to the size of the tatami, the straw mats that traditionally covered interior floors. To keep his metallic lines from seeming perfect (which would be considered a fault, since, as Japanese design recognizes, true perfection is unobtainable), Herman has allowed the moss to creep over the bronze here and there to shatter the grid's tyranny.

Taken all together, Herman says, this garden is an exploration of "how you move through space. You get to look at things in bits and pieces before you actually get to them. It's a series of scenes unfolding like a play." Herman finds precedents for this in Japanese garden design, though the suspicion is unavoidable that another aspect of his personal history may have played a part. You imagine the young nurseryman in the back lots of Hollywood; it's not surprising that there is a cinematographic quality to the garden he has made, that the perspectives and the shots have been so carefully plotted.

"Students must learn," says Ron Herman of his classes at Berkeley, "that the path to modernity is through the past." Spend enough time in contemplation of the garden he made for Larry Ellison, and the statement becomes clear.

OPPOSITE
Ron Herman united East and West, the traditional with the utterly modern, to create a unique and unforgettable space.

ROGER WARNER
California

"his hill was a hot, dry, nasty place where you got stickers in
your socks," says Roger Warner, describing this Napa Valley
enclave. Not surprisingly, the new owners, Dick and Pam
Kramlich, wanted to change that. They, and Warner, had ambitions. "The basic California garden keeps out rattlesnakes and provides shade. We wanted to do more than that here."

They wanted quite a lot, actually. They wanted not only shade
and security, but also color and serenity. The Kramlichs wanted a
place to entertain; Warner wanted somehow to integrate an informal
garden with the relentless geometry of the surrounding vineyards.

"Simplify and repeat" was the formula Warner arrived at. He
has impeccable credentials as a plantsman—he had worked and
studied for a number of years with two masters, Marshall Olbrich
and Lester Hawkins of the legendary Western Hills Rare Plants
Nursery in Occidental, California. During the late 1970s and
through the 1980s, Olbrich and Hawkins had reinvented the garden floras of northern California, importing a flood of choice specimens from the Mediterranean basin, Australia, and South Africa.

Warner had absorbed their enthusiasm, then learned to temper
it. Warner retains a sense of gratitude for what these two "wild and
crazy guys" shared with him. They showed him that "gardens
could be art." Eventually he developed reservations about what he
describes as their habit of design by the "shotgun effect. You load
it up with plants, and blast the landscape."

Warner has learned to master his exhaustive knowledge of
plants to select the one that will bring out the best in a site. He has

"When I like a plant, I want to be bathed in it."
—ROGER WARNER

learned that the repetition of a few elements can, if handled skill-fully, establish harmony and a powerful sense of unity.

In the Kramlichs' garden, he selected a palette of gray-green, white, and purple. "Too many colors and forms are exhausting," he notes. Then he chose the plants that would be the backbone of the design. The Kramlichs liked the four dogwoods already on the site, so Warner planted another forty, establishing an understory through the native oak woodland. He seeded broad swaths of purple-blossomed foxgloves, *Scilla peruviana*, and *Salvia* 'Purple Rain,' drifts of white-flowered clary sage, explosions of euphorbias and sea oats with silver-tongued *Stachys* 'Helen von Stein.'

To structure this unabashedly romantic planting, and to build a transition to the vineyards, another designer might well have fallen back on an architectural device. The easiest way to deal with such a discordant view is to turn your back on it, to screen it out with a fence or a wall. Warner refused to settle for this. He decided to use plants from the garden's palette in a sculptural way, to bring order to the garden's core while also embracing the sweeping valley vistas.

Warner installed his own grid around the garden's periphery. Starting at the entrance, he planted a fan of lavender, clipped into hemispheres and planted in neatly spaced and ruled rows. The result of this, he says, was to create "a point of view." The Kram-lichs and their guests can relax at the garden's core without feeling exposed, yet still feel included in the countryside.

Warner's originality as a designer stems, in part, from his lack of formal training. He does not have a degree in landscape archi-tecture indeed, he has never taken a class. Rather, he has learned by what he calls "paying attention": by observing and doing, then looking again to assess the results. "I think someone has to have some innate ability. Then you have to slap it around, wake it up."

Garden design is always a partnership in Warner's view, and he is quite frank about the aesthetic debt he owes his clients. In a prac-tical sense, their tastes should shape the landscape. Creating a gar-den, Warner elaborates, is "like making slippers for the client; it has to fit." Ideally, the interactions become something much more than taking the client's measure. Ideally, patron and designer play off of each other to create something better than either had envisioned.

OPPOSITE

Warner broadcast seed of foxglove to create groves of the spiked flowers. "When you have a good plant," he explains, "you should use it in profu-sion to get a grand effect."

ABOVE

Rocks from the vineyard were used to build the wall that encloses the garden.

LEFT

Intermingled drifts of euphorbias, Nepeta 'Six Hills Giant,' and Scilla peruviana offer many textures and shades of green under a canopy of native oaks.

In this respect, the Kramlichs definitely raised the stakes. Their sophisticated interest in the arts—the Kramlichs are benefactors of the San Francisco Museum of Modern Art—gave them high standards but also an openness to unconventional ideas. Pam Kramlich, in particular, had a profound effect on the garden's planting. She is a collector of video art, Warner notes, and is especially "sensitive to color and form."

"She had certain preferences," Warner explains, "and as we began to work with the plant material, [these] began to reveal themselves. By restricting the palette, you create interesting effects. It [the garden] became more of an art form than a flower garden."

As a work of art, this garden is more like a Frankenthaler than a Miró. There are no hard edges here. Warner's goal was a garden that would "ooze over the hilltop," and he has lapped the space with wave after wave of succulents, herbs, perennials, and velvety turf. The planting rises in layers: grassy floor, nepeta at your knees, euphorbia waist high, clematis and white roses twining into the oaks overhead.

Simplify and repeat. "When you have a good plant," Warner says, "you should use it in profusion to get a grand effect. When I like a plant, I want to be bathed in it. This is what makes a garden calming. If you use a little here and there, the garden will be exhausting. Most gardens make me want to take a nap."

By any standard, the Kramlich garden is exceptional. But then, says Warner, it was an exceptional partnership—of site, plants, setting, and above all clients. That is the essential. "The education and the taste of the patron is equally important as the ability of the artist," Warner states. "It's not very often you can create great gardens. The clients aren't up to it."

OPPOSITE
White clary sage and Salvia *'Purple Rain' (rear) are the backdrop for an eddy of boulders overrun with baby's tears.*

OVERLEAF
In a garden virtually without architectural elements, boldly clipped plants (lavender and teucrium) and the rugged verticals of the oak trunks supply the essential structure.

TOPHER DELANEY

California

I ask them where they spent their first six years on the planet.
I ask them what do they remember about where they grew up.
What color? What was the terrain like? Where was their bed-
room? What did they do outside and with whom did they do it?
Were there secret places that they loved? Places that they were
fearful of?"

Topher Delaney is listing the questions she poses to clients before
she begins the design process. She's trying to understand the culture
with which she must collaborate. "I view clients as cultures,"
Delaney explains. This might seem peculiar, except that before she
took her degree in landscape architecture she studied cultural
anthropology. She also studied philosophy, while pursuing painting,
drawing, and sculpture. All these enthusiasms and disciplines combine in Delaney's design to give it an extraordinary richness.

Delaney's gardens spring from so many inspirations that to
assign them to a single school or movement is, ultimately, impossible. Cerebral, sensual, and spiritual, they have many faces. Yet in
their clean aesthetic and innovative use of man-made materials—
concrete, stone, glass, and steel—and their fearless, often playful,
abstraction, these gardens certainly rate as modernist. It might be
more accurate to classify them not as examples of modernism but
rather as a challenge to modernism, a suggestion of how far it
might go, had it the imagination and the nerve.

Delaney speaks much of "metaphor," an element whose importance in her design runs directly counter to contemporary trends
in the United States. The current focus, Delaney notes, is over-

OPPOSITE

The deep, soft Mexican feather grass
in the Gennet garden exemplifies the
healing, nurturing character of
Topher Delaney's design.

"I ask them where they spent their first six years on the planet. What did they do outside…? Were there secret places that they loved?"

—TOPHER DELANEY

whelmingly on whether the garden looks good, which is impor- tant. But allegory and metaphor are also important, in her opinion, and they are too often absent nowadays.

To illustrate what she means, Delaney cites the scholars' gar- dens of Suzhou, China. Legacies of the imperial era, these were designed as places meant to work on the visitor's consciousness and help him go inward and rise to another level. "An intervention into the tissue of life," Delaney calls them, something, she adds, that modern designers rarely attempt, at least not deliberately.

Delaney does, and she is forthright about this. In the play space she created as part of a series of urban enclosures for one San Francisco family stand three rocks. For the children they offer an opportunity for climbing. To adults they are a deliberate reference to the baroque stones in those Suzhou scholars' gardens. The Chi- nese originals were pillars of water-eroded limestone raised from the floor of Lake T'ai Hu; Delaney found a similarly figured piece of California marble and then sculpted the other two from a dark gray concrete. These rocks have a brooding presence that contrasts dramatically with the toys of simple form and bright color scat- tered all around; after finishing the adventure of the rocks, the children can retreat to the gaiety of the circular sandbox filled with pink sand and set on casters so that it can be moved about.

There is a more grown-up area (chronologically speaking) just a short climb to an elevated deck with a magnificent vista of the San Francisco Bay. Nature's cycles also fascinate Delaney, and she has captured the daily progression of the light by setting panels of dichroic glass into the transparent windscreen that surrounds the deck. This glass changes color not only as the viewer moves around the deck but also as the sun transits across the sky, re-coloring the view minute by minute from sunrise to sunset.

The language Delaney uses to define her work highlights her intellectual interests, but there is also a pervasive spirituality to her design. This is most obvious in the healing gardens that she has created for a number of hospitals; they are the result of an informal pact she made with herself when struggling with breast cancer in the mid 1980s, that if she survived she would put her art in the service of healing others. The spiritual vein runs through all she does—one only has to learn to find it.

Delaney refers to another urban garden as "the garden of reve-lation." She insists that it should be experienced sequentially. "A garden is a descent from one space to another in an exploration of the choice between light and dark, the passive and the active, both in our environment and in our life," she says. You find the alterna-tives counterpoised at the very entrance to the garden, where a steel-framed gate of sandblasted glass permits the passage of light but robs the view of detail so that the identity of forms on the other side is lost. Fiber optics light the pool in the entry court, and you step down the stairs to a central plaza paneled with opaque glass that glows with increasing intensity as darkness falls.

In this scene the brushwork is bold but largely intangible. That is a choice, though, for Delaney expresses herself just as easily in the tactile, as she has proved with a garden in Napa. There, on the dry uplands, grassland is the "cycle," the natural habitat, and Delaney has planted around the house and the pool a stand of Mexican feather grass (*Stipa tenuissima*), golden tufts so deep and soft you cannot see them without wanting to stroke them, to run

ABOVE
Simple lines give an iconographic impact to the details. Inlaid into the dry grassland like a rectangle of lapis lazuli, the pool becomes more than a place to swim.

A pittosporum shades the stylized spring Delaney assembled by fitting a chadar, an antique Indian cascade, into the stainless-steel frame.

your fingers through them as through a mane of golden hair.

Water is the most precious commodity in this setting, and Delaney has centered her elegant plantings around a swimming pool. On one level, this is, perhaps, another metaphor; the pool is a mirror for the sky and it is the spring at the heart of the sanctuary—though one can certainly enjoy the refreshment of a swim without taking a spiritual plunge. Delaney knows the importance of physical gratification—the elegant black basin she set beside the dining area is decorative, but it is intended to furnish the family dogs with a drink whenever they need one. Delaney doesn't limit her planning to the needs of bipeds.

That, in the end, is what makes the gardens of Topher Delaney irresistible. The intellectual challenges posed by this learned and irrepressible woman bring growth and excitement, but there are certain times when we do not feel equal to the challenge. We can feel her gardens' spirituality when we need healing, but again, there will surely be occasions when that is also more than we want. Who, though, will refuse a cool drink on a hot, dry day; a view of the bay filtered through sun-tinted glass; or the comfort of light as darkness falls? We will find these things in the landscape of Topher Delaney— these interventions that she makes into the tissue of our lives.

ABOVE
As darkness falls, backlighting causes the glass panels enclosing this court to glow with increasing intensity.

OPPOSITE
In a characteristically whimsical touch, Delaney backed the cascade with a mirror to reflect light down onto the planting bed.

ABOVE

Panels of dichroic glass in the screen around this viewing deck change color with the transit of the sun.

OPPOSITE

To echo the infinite variety of blues in San Francisco Bay, Delaney had an Italian artist, Tania Saderi, create an abstract mosaic, a wall of polished plaster panels of thirty-two hues.

OVERLEAF

This elegant black basin is decorative, and functional too, providing a drink for the dogs whenever they need it.

ACKNOWLEDGMENTS

*Our thanks for their support to S. I. Newhouse, James Truman,
Charles Townsend, John Bellando, and Anthony Petrillose*

*For beautiful work in and out of the garden,
Tom Christopher, Charlotte Frieze, Senga Mortimer, Deborah
Needleman, Stephen Orr, Carolina Irving, and Melissa Ozawa*

*A good book rests on vigilant attention to quality and detail for
which we thank Elizabeth Pochoda, Anthony Jazzar,
Lucy Gilmour, Stephen Orr, Betsey Barnum, Trent Farmer,
Alice Siempelkamp, Greg Wustefeld, John R. Shepherd,
and Elisabeth Rietvelt*

*And our gratitude to our friends at the
New York Botanical Garden and the Garden Conservancy
for their advice and wisdom over the years*